Networlding

The Jossey-Bass
Business & Management Series

Networlding

Building Relationships and Opportunities for Success

Melissa Giovagnoli

Jocelyn Carter-Miller

 JOSSEY-BASS
A Wiley Company
San Francisco

Jossey-Bass books and products are available through most bookstores. To contact Jossey-Bass directly, call (888) 378-2537, fax to (800) 605-2665, or visit our website at www.josseybass.com.

Substantial discounts on bulk quantities of Jossey-Bass books are available to corporations, professional associations, and other organizations. For details and discount information, contact the special sales department at Jossey-Bass.

TCF Manufactured in the United States of America on Lyons Falls Turin Book. This paper is acid-free and 100 percent totally chlorine-free.

Library of Congress Cataloging-in-Publication Data

Giovagnoli, Melissa.
      Networlding: building relationships and opportunities for success /
      Melissa Giovagnoli, Jocelyn Carter-Miller.—1st ed.
         p. cm.—(The Jossey-Bass business & management series)
         ISBN 0-7879-4819-5 (acid-free paper)
      1. Business networks. 2. Strategic alliances (Business) I. Carter-Miller, Jocelyn. II. Title.
   III. Series.
      HD69.S8 G56 2000
      650.1'3—dc21   00–008480

FIRST EDITION
HB Printing   10 9 8 7 6 5 4 3 2 1

Contents

To God, whose greatest gift to us is each other, which allows us to create endless opportunities for all, if we could but realize the power of this gift
—M.G.

To Berneice Carter, my mother, who is my role model and first connection; Joshua Carter, my father, who is my strongest supporter; Kimberly Carter, my sister, who is my dream-catcher; Alexis and Kimberly Miller, my daughters, who are my inspiration; and Edward Miller, my husband, who is my best friend and life's guide
—J.C.M.

Preface
Simple Tales of Success and Fulfillment

When we met a couple of years ago in serving on the Women's Advisory Board at the University of Chicago Graduate School of Business, we knew that we had similar beliefs and passions. We really cared about making it easier for people to connect with each other and with the resources needed to reach their goals. We believed that in a fast-changing world, the ability to network effectively and create mutually beneficial opportunities was essential for success. We called this ability *Networlding*.

Backgrounds and Purpose

In our own words, we each want to share with you our simple tales of success and fulfillment through Networlding.

Melissa Giovagnoli's Tale

I took a different path from Jocelyn's but ended up in a very similar place, realizing that when it comes to making opportunities work, it's people first. I have been an entrepreneur for more than a decade, and I find that the freedom and creativity it offers fill my spirit. I've also been Networlding now for more than seven years and have found that it's an amazing process, a transformational one.

When Jocelyn and I met, I knew we both had a goal of making a difference. We saw the potential connection between our personal relationship and our professional interests in reaching that goal.

Today, as a result of our commitment to the Networlding process, in which we both believe so strongly, we have together created a book that is truly more than the sum of the two of us. There is real power in the pages that follow, given to us by the divine source that we both acknowledge. We want to share this gift that we've received with you, and we hope that you will take it and do what all great networlders would do: pass it on!

Jocelyn Carter-Miller's Tale

For many years, I have climbed the elusive corporate ladder—and by an outsider's view, I've been successful. I have been a consultant, a marketing vice president, and an international general manager for premier companies. But it wasn't until recently that I gained a real seat at the table, a chair among the exclusive power elite. Over the last few years, my career has suddenly gained tremendous traction and taken off at warp speed! Suddenly, I have a choice of careers, circumstances, and rewards. I've experienced both career success and fulfillment.

I did it not by hard work and results alone, nor by the "4 Ps"— that is, preparing, plotting, performing, and pleading. I did it by thinking differently, by transforming how I viewed myself and my career, by collaborating, by Networlding. I must have been asked countless times how I got the opportunity to teach at the university level without a Ph.D., how I was able to write and publish a book with limited previous experience, how I was chosen for a plum corporate assignment—and didn't even have to relocate my family. My answer is always the same. I did it by mobilizing my networld around developing new opportunities from which all the parties involved benefit.

That's why I had to write this book. I have to tell every one of you the secret that has taken me so long to figure out *and* to put into practice. The secret is Networlding: collaborating for shared opportunity, success, and fulfillment.

In the new twenty-first century workplace, our careers often resemble games of checkers, with job moves taking us sideways, backwards, or even out of the game before we eventually go forward. Our next assignment or project is likely to be based on who we know, who knows us, and what resources we bring rather than our track records or company affiliations. In this environment, Networlding is the fundamental skill we need to succeed. For you and for me, the stakes in understanding and embracing Networlding are high because it's so closely linked to our ability to achieve our goals, choose our careers, and realize our own rewards. It is, perhaps, our only safety net.

Sharing the Networlding concept with you has been a journey of discovery, learning, and appreciation. I've discovered that there are underlying connections among everyone and everything in our new, connected society. I've learned that by making my intent known to those I value, and who in turn value me, I can activate an entire support system to create new opportunities and accomplish my goals. Most important, I have come to appreciate the resourcefulness and willingness of those people in my life who move mountains to help me move forward. For me, Networlding has proven to be much more than a new and critical collaborative skill. It has become my path—as it will for you—to success and fulfillment.

Audience for This Book

Because Networlding is the fundamental new skill needed for success in today's connected society, this book is an indispensable resource for everyone in every industry or nonprofit organization, at any stage of his or her career, who is interested in advancing. Whether you're an executive, consultant, administrative assistant, or freelancer, you can benefit from understanding the principles and tools of Networlding for building mutually beneficial relationships and new opportunities that align with your goals.

As a guide for establishing the effective people-and-opportunity network you need to get ahead, this book is particularly useful if you are starting out or midway through your career. Whether you are seeking a career opportunity in a small organization or a large corporation, starting a new business, or building an independent professional practice, you can use Networlding skills to connect with potential employers and customers to identify new jobs or careers, or to obtain the information and resources required by an innovative endeavor.

Although geared to you as an individual reader, your organization will find Networlding a successful approach for building internal teams across departments, sharing information and knowledge, and forming external strategic alliances that lead to higher growth and satisfaction.

Overview

Working and living in the twenty-first century, with such broad access to highly valued information and innovation, is very exciting because you essentially have the ability to create your own future. It's also daunting for the very same reason. However, if you really understand what's required of this new working environment and your underlying connection to other people and resources, you are then able to define your own career path, create the right opportunities, and position yourself to succeed.

As you read this book, you will learn that positioning yourself for success means fully developing and leveraging your network—that group of individuals from all areas of your life, perhaps stretching from one end of the globe to the other, with whom you are connected because you share similar intent, values, goals, and interests. The chapters that follow walk you through the Networlding concept and the comprehensive seven-step process for effective Networlding (see Figure 1).

Chapters One and Two explain exactly what we mean when we talk about Networlding; they present the golden rules that underlie this process. They examine the basic Networlding concept and what it can mean for you, and—importantly—how it differs from networking, which is a less value-driven process. Chapter One offers a quiz for you to assess your Networlding skills, and it also introduces the support exchange model, which summarizes and illustrates the essential building blocks for developing strong relationships and opportunities using the Networlding process. Chapter Two provides the principles of Networlding and an understanding of why this process will work for you.

In Chapters Three through Nine we describe the proven seven-step process illustrated in Figure 1 that you must follow to build the relationships and opportunities that enable you to reach your goals much faster, while experiencing greater fulfillment in the process. Each of these chapters explains one step in detail, reveals the rationale that makes the step work, and provides real-life examples. The exercises included in each chapter guide you in developing your networlds and improving your skills. Taken together, the seven steps constitute a powerful system for success in today's new network society. The system also brings "far out" goals within reach:

Figure 1. Networlding: Building Personal and Professional Relationships for Success.

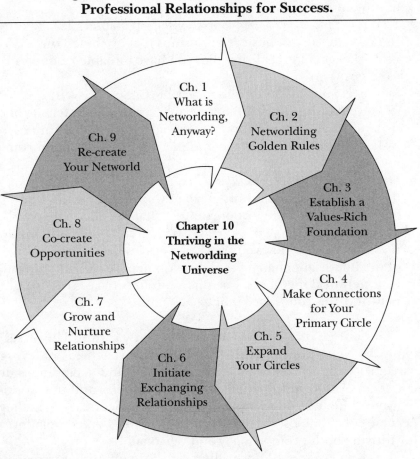

- Step one: *establish a values-rich foundation* (Chapter Three). Determine what matters most to you, define your personal charter, set your goals, and develop your plan for achieving them.
- Step two: *make connections for your primary circle* (Chapter Four). Assess your potential relationships from a basis of values as well as business, cognitive, and emotional factors. Find those networld partners who will yield deep connections, contribute to your professional life, and enrich your personal life as well.
- Step three: *expand your circles* (Chapter Five) Grow your primary circle, or strongest relationships, by adding those

individuals who demonstrate the traits of networlders and act as influencers.

- Step four: *initiate exchanging relationships* (Chapter Six). Take the initiative to establish relationships that are based on mutual exchange, realizing that you have valuable resources to offer others.
- Step five: *grow and nurture relationships* (Chapter Seven). Achieve the vibrant, collaborative exchanges characteristic of dynamic networlds, which produce significant opportunities by learning to use specific techniques for growing and nurturing your relationships.
- Step six: *co-create opportunities* (Chapter Eight). Leverage your talents in combination with those in your networld to create joint and boundaryless opportunities that benefit all involved.
- Step seven: *re-create your networld* (Chapter Nine). Continuously reevaluate and renew your networld circles by staying on top of the important changes and developments experienced by your networld members. Use this awareness to re-create your networld and your place in it.

The last chapter, "Thriving in the Networlding Universe," explores Networlding as more than an approach to achieving career success; it's a way of life. We share how understanding your connections to diverse people and opportunities, and transforming your thinking and approach to those connections so that they become collaboration for shared gain, offer you a greater platform for thriving both professionally and personally.

It is your personal Networlding transformation that paves the way for you to accept the next wave in the evolution of our new, connected society. This wave is actually more than a milestone; it's a revolution in modern society's holistic evolvement toward the professional, community, and personal growth of its participants. To evolve holistically means to let go of our old, comfortable strategies for achieving success, and sometimes to rely on higher insight. It means choosing the road less traveled, embracing Networlding. Though you may find it scary at first, adopting these collaborative Networlding strategies will inevitably produce a deeper and richer demonstration of your intent, and a faster route to your goals. They will place you firmly in the Networlding universe.

This is because the essence of Networlding is its appeal to our inherent connectedness to each other and passion for our causes. This connectedness and passion create fertile ground for developing new opportunities that lead to success and resultant rewards of deep, personal fulfillment. As a result of your connecting and exchanging with others who also use Networlding strategies for getting ahead, you tap into the rhythm of universal purpose—benefiting yourself, your networld, and, even more important, your community and ultimately the entire world.

We wish you much growth and success on your Networlding journey.

April 2000

MELISSA GIOVAGNOLI
Schaumburg, Illinois
JOCELYN CARTER-MILLER
Parkland, Florida

Acknowledgments

My deepest thanks to the many people who helped create this book. Following are their names: Joyce Watts, who introduced me to Jeanne Thompson; Jeanne Thompson, who introduced me to Susan Miner; Susan Miner, who introduced me to Jocelyn during a meeting of the University of Chicago Graduate Business Women's Advisory Board, where we met as board members; Joe Palumbo, who introduced me to Jackie Sloane, positioning coach; Eileen McDargh, speaking professional; Mike Galiga of Kohl's Department Stores; Sue Baeckler; Nancy Burgess; Christine Corelli, speaking professional; Susan Fignar of Image Works Wonders; Margo Pachona of Connections Unlimited Speakers Bureau in Chicago; Chad Coe and his referral group, ReferGroup.com; Debra Zahay; Vince Racioppo, coauthor of the Networlding quiz, at the Center for Expert Performance; Brent Stewart of Brent Stewart & Associates; the team at ReferNet.com; Cheryl and Michael Kuhlman, good friends who introduced me to Participate.com; the team at Participate.com; Julie Seeley of Loretto Conference Center in Wheaton, Illinois, and all the wonderful nuns who were Networlding over a century ago; Denham Turton, president of WhoYouKnow.com; the team at ivillage.com; the team at Sixdegrees.com; Larry Mohl of Motorola University and a great knowledge-sharing colleague; Bruce Wexler, who introduced me to Cedric Crocker; Cedric Crocker, who introduced me to the wonderful team at Jossey-Bass; Cheryl Greenway at Jossey-Bass; Cari Auger, my sister; Cindy Goodman, my sister; Greg Goodman, my brother; Steve, my supportive husband; Graham and Gavin, my great Networlding sons; and the thousands of networlders who helped perfect the Networlding process over the past decade.
—M.G.

I would like to acknowledge with gratitude the following important people who encouraged, supported, and contributed to the development of Networlding—both the concept and the book—and me: Edward Miller, Blanche Templeton, Linda Lanton, Rachelle Franklin, Naomi Endo, Dwight Bernard, Bonita Miller, Jose Figueroa, Vesna Arsic, Bill Wiggenhorn, Darab Unwalla, Leon Garza, Keith Bane, Earle Markes, Janiece Webb, Betsy Bernard, Bob Growney, Chris Galvin, Pat Canovan, Randy Bryant, Roberta Pryzbilski Michel Levy, Arial Shapiro, Eduardo Conrado, Juan Luna, Guillermo Monroy, Edgardo Cruz, Alberto Hoffman, Sheila Griffin, John Hassett, Susan Hooker, Jim Winski, Evelyn Luxgang, John Lynch, Tom Crawford, Greg Nelson, Bob Schaul, Geoffrey Frost, Bob Bigony, Gus Arenas, Lenny Debarros, Carlos Genardini, Carlos Barrodelo, Eva Boswell, James Palmer, Deveta Peoples, Ruth Peoples, Dorothy and Ivory Carr, Marrietta and James Palmer, Verbatine Palmer, Jason Palmer, Shari and Booker Vance, Darryl Carr, Louise and Mc Glother Irving, James and Lorraine Irving, Doris Irvin, Ida and Edward Miller, Dawn Miller, Jean and Paul Miller, Jerrold and Joyce Miller, and my many other friends, colleagues, and relatives who make up my extended networld.

I also would like to thank my coauthor, editors, and publishers—Melissa Giovagnoli, Bruce Wexler, Cheryl Greenway, and Cedric Crocker, respectively—for making this a remarkable experience and a memorable book.

—J.C.M.

About the Authors

Melissa Giovagnoli is the author or coauthor of six other successful books, including *75 Cage-Rattling Questions That Change the Way You Work; The Power of Two: How Companies of All Sizes Can Build Alliance Networks That Generate Business Opportunities;* and *Angels in the Workplace: Stories and Inspirations for Creating a New World of Work.*

For over seventeen years she has been helping individuals and corporations understand Networlding, the powerful process she created almost a decade ago that accelerates both personal and organizational growth through coaching and mentoring. In today's world, where the network is quickly becoming the dominant form of organizational development, she offers a unique and effective system for achieving twenty-first century growth.

Giovagnoli has been a guest on both radio and television, including CNN, WGN, CNBC, and FOX channels, and her books have been featured on "Oprah Winfrey" and "The Today Show." Her clients include Price Waterhouse, KPMG, AT&T, and Humana Hospitals, as well as dozens of smaller companies and organizations. She is a frequent presenter at conferences that wish to include interactive sessions. Her unique Networlding program has been highly evaluated by Meeting Professionals International (MPI).

After obtaining a B.A. in sociology and a J.D. from DePaul University College of Law, she went on to found Service Showcase, an innovative training and consulting firm that is now in its fourteenth year. She has also been an international speaker for more than seven years. She recently created networlding.com, the first directory for socially responsible businesses and consumers. She lives with her husband and two children in Schaumburg, Illinois.

Jocelyn Carter-Miller, a practitioner of Networlding in the real world, has built a successful career using higher-order networking to create new opportunities for corporations, nonprofit organizations, and individuals.

Earlier in her career, as the founder of Carter-Miller Enterprises, a marketing and creative consulting firm for the entertainment industry, she realized the power of connecting diverse industries, community organizations, and people to gain access to new resources and achieve goals. She employed these skills while vice president of marketing and product development for Mattel, where she broke new ground, driving record sales of Barbie and other toys with integrated product, entertainment, promotional, and licensing programs.

Currently, Carter-Miller is corporate vice president and chief marketing officer of Motorola, a global provider of integrated communications solutions and embedded electronic solutions with annual sales over $30 billion. As CMO, she has helped build the Motorola brand and image and driven high-performance marketing organizations and processes. She also heads motorola.com, the Motorola electronic commerce and information Web site. In her previous roles, she managed international wireless communications network operations for Motorola in Latin American and European countries, creating profitable opportunities through strategic alliances, value-added applications, and new product and service launches.

She continues to build strong relationships and new opportunities through her involvement with corporate boards and nonprofit organizations. She has won numerous awards, been featured in national publications, and regularly addresses business and community groups. She obtained her M.B.A. in marketing and finance at the University of Chicago and her B.S. in accounting at the University of Illinois, Urbana-Champaign, and is a certified public accountant. She is married to Edward Miller, president of Edventures, an educational reform and development firm, and has two daughters, Alexis and Kimberly.

Giovagnoli and Carter-Miller have created networlding.com, the first directory for socially responsible individuals and businesses. Through their networlding.com Web site, they facilitate meaningful connections and mutually beneficial opportunities for novice and expert networlders alike.

Networlding

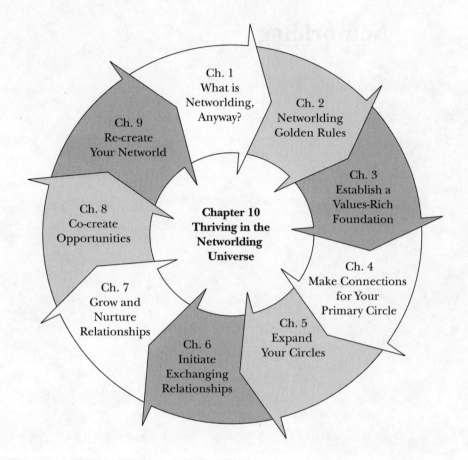

Ch. 1
What is
Networlding,
Anyway?

Ch. 2
Networlding
Golden Rules

Ch. 3
Establish a
Values-Rich
Foundation

Ch. 4
Make Connections
for Your
Primary Circle

Ch. 5
Expand
Your Circles

Ch. 6
Initiate
Exchanging
Relationships

Ch. 7
Grow and
Nurture
Relationships

Ch. 8
Co-create
Opportunities

Ch. 9
Re-create
Your Networld

Chapter 10
Thriving in the
Networlding
Universe

CHAPTER ONE

What Is Networlding, Anyway?

Networlding is a transforming concept in a world where connections to everyone and everything really count. It provides us with a fresh vision of how to move forward in our lives and careers, a vision that is very much in keeping with our rapidly changing environment. Networlding is rooted in our connected society of information technology and the Internet, where we measure our accomplishments by a new yardstick—not just by pay and promotions. Instead, we look to gain new skills and experiences and want to work on fun, exciting projects with people we respect and like. We perform our jobs in our offices and while on the move. We teleconference and share knowledge with a broad, perhaps even global, group of colleagues. For many of us, the line between personal and professional blurs, and some of us are hard-pressed to differentiate between work and fun.

Peter Drucker asked his MBA students what they would call this connected society, and they responded, "We'd call it the New Network Society." That's close but not quite it. *Network* suggests a traditional model of connections, but we've evolved beyond this tradition. Network connections are often superficial, and we're seeing people connect in ways that are far deeper and more meaningful. We all have the potential to make incredible linkages with each other and to leverage these linkages in powerful ways. To do so, we need to understand how we are all connected and how to use these connections for mutual gain. Just as importantly, we must make a dramatic shift in our professional and personal strategies for getting ahead. This shift is from a "me" perspective to the more leveraged "we" perspective, and it means forming and maintaining relationships in radically different ways.

Networlding is the strategy that will allow you to achieve these ambitious objectives. It facilitates your developing multilevel connections with others and creating new opportunities that benefit yourself, your colleagues, and your community. Networlding goes well beyond the traditional relationship-building techniques of networking and fits into the fluid, almost organic nature of our new world of work. Let's examine what Networlding is, especially in the context of what networking has been.

Networlding Versus Networking

Certainly there is a passing resemblance between Networlding and networking—both revolve around the concept of forming relationships. But the resemblance ends as soon as you understand that Networlding requires clear intent, compatible values, reciprocal exchange and support, and mutually developed, mutually beneficial outcomes.

Networlding is a purposeful process of collaboration that not only achieves mutual goals but also leads to professional and personal fulfillment. In contrast, networking is an often haphazard process of making contacts to achieve short-term and often one-sided goals. In addition, Networlding is opportunity-expansive, whereas networking is opportunity-specific. This means that in a networld relationship a series of opportunities flow from the partnership, whereas in a network relationship people come together to take advantage of a specific opportunity at best. The differences between the two concepts become clear when you consider the experiences of Robert, a consummate networker, and those of Bonita, a Networlding maven.

Robert began his career during college when he became a waiter in a prestigious hotel. Because of his outgoing nature and ability to provide superb service, he was a favorite of hotel guests. When Robert wanted a higher-paying job with a good future, he began asking around. One of the guests offered him a sales position. With his contacts and service orientation, he quickly became very successful. He then set his sights on a business that he could own. He became a respected publishing entrepreneur who today knows most of the community and business leaders in his area.

Robert is never without his networking tool kit—business cards, organizer, and promotional giveaways—because he never knows when or where a new referral may take place. His contacts have enabled him to keep abreast of local stories and to attract a consistent set of advertisers. Yet he has not received the necessary support to expand his media empire in the ways he would like, and the time he has invested in his constant networking has also hurt his relationships with close family and friends.

Despite his networking success, Robert is dissatisfied. Part of the problem is his insecurity and guilt. He feels uncomfortable about having "used" people to get what he wanted while giving them relatively little in return. Although he has a vast number of relationships, very few are of the quality he would like. His contacts have helped him achieve entrepreneurial goals, but those goals quickly lost their luster. Robert hoped for much more than his networking success has provided. He harbored dreams of expanding his publishing business into other media, especially the Internet; he always wanted to be a leader in his field and introduce new ideas and innovations to publishing. Just as important, Robert hoped to find like-minded people in his field with whom he could build something new and worthwhile. Sometimes when talking to his business partners and direct reports, he has felt that people are only listening to him because they have to. There is no real sense of connection, and as a result Robert has found it difficult to be open with them and to engage in dialogues that are energizing and highly productive. In the last few years, Robert has found himself merely going through the motions, and his lack of attention and emotional involvement has hurt his publishing business.

Now let's contrast Robert's experiences with those of a networlder. Bonita, who is skilled at math and finances, was always driven by a desire to help the economically disadvantaged achieve financial stability. After college, Bonita found a job in a small accounting firm in New York. She convinced the firm that it was in their interest to support her professional and community activities because it would also mean additional business and recruiting opportunities for them. Through her formal and informal activities, Bonita realized that the poor could benefit greatly from expense management advice and investment education. She needed to identify and connect with individuals who could help provide this type of information.

Bonita pursued relationships with investment-savvy individuals who were also community-oriented. Before meeting with each of these individuals she clearly thought about the potential opportunities and benefits that both of them would be likely to realize from their relationship. She knew that just passing out her card was a waste of time and wanted instead to establish relationships with people who not only possessed the requisite skills but shared her beliefs. After contacting and meeting them, Bonita nurtured and strengthened these relationships by regularly giving and receiving emotional support as well as information.

Many opportunities flowed from these relationships. Bonita was able to help the disadvantaged in ways that continue to expand in new directions, including offering financial seminars for the poor and making television and radio talk show appearances. At the same time, she introduced the influential people who assisted her to each other, and they pursued projects of mutual interest. Bonita also helped some of her connections learn that they could do good work and make money simultaneously, and this realization was gratifying to everyone in Bonita's networld. It should come as no surprise that Bonita now has her own highly successful investment firm and partners with different people to put on seminars for the economically disadvantaged around the country.

Bonita used Networlding to create mutually beneficial opportunities that fit with her sense of purpose. As the new opportunities and benefits emerged, she expanded her circle to include others. Bonita understood the connections between her intentions, values, opportunities, and other people, and this is what helped her and her networld succeed in ways that would not have been possible if she'd taken a networking path.

Apples and Oranges: Specific Distinctions Between Networlding and Networking

Bonita's and Robert's experiences are clearly different, but the differences between Networlding and networking are not always so easily understood. Part of the problem is that there is some overlap; both involve trying to meet influential people who can help in some way. Let's examine Networlding and networking in detail so that the two become distinct concepts.

Intent is a key word in Networlding. We use it to mean forming relationships and opportunities intentionally—being highly conscious about the underlying values, goals, and beliefs that drive you toward a specific relationship or opportunity. Your intent may be to obtain a specific job or to establish a certain type of business but it is also to know what beliefs and values are important to you as you pursue these goals.

Dwight, a networlder, is a successful educator in his mid-thirties. His intent was to improve the education of disadvantaged youths. He was intensely aware that he valued education, that he believed it was an underutilized tool in poor communities, and that there was a need to apply it in more imaginative, aggressive ways. Dwight identified a series of goals that would need to be met in order to realize his intent and also identified people who shared his values and beliefs and could help him achieve the goals. With the support of community, businesses, and other educators, Dwight created a new curriculum, instructional method, and school design that significantly improved students' academic performance and self-esteem.

The intent in Networlding is thus multidimensional. In contrast, networking is one-dimensional, focused on achieving one goal by making the right contacts. The multidimensionality in Networlding involves goals that are linked to values and beliefs. You need to form relationships that encompass more than one factor. It may be that your values demand you fulfill not one but a series of goals; you may have to search for people with both the disparate skills and shared beliefs necessary to achieve successive goals.

Networlding doesn't happen by accident. You must identify and communicate your intent to make something happen. In a highly purposeful manner, you must keep your dream in mind as you search for and form relationships.

It's also important to understand that while networking can be a selfish activity, Networlding is not a completely selfless endeavor either. You enter into Networlding relationships recognizing that they involve a continuous exchange of information, ideas, opportunities, and support. Friends, colleagues, and associates who are attracted to this idea of exchange will help you achieve your goals as you help them achieve theirs.

Usually, Networlding relationships start when you clearly express your intent in the broad sense. Quickly and convincingly, you communicate your goals and values, and when you do, people who resonate to your intent will respond. This requires taking some risk—you're revealing who you are and risking rejection. But you're also playing for higher stakes than in networking. If someone responds positively and you are able to establish a Networlding relationship, you can reap tremendous benefits. Your new partner will not only provide you with more opportunities but also provide an empathic ear and a source of fresh ideas.

Networking exists on a much more superficial level. In most instances, networkers use a scattergun approach to develop many contacts and referrals. The theory is that the more contacts they make, the greater the odds that one will pay off. As a result, networking is a time-consuming and frustrating activity. With networking, you spend most of your time not achieving your goals because you're not searching intentionally. It's like going out on blind dates or making cold calls; you figure if you do an activity enough, it will eventually yield something of value. It might, but only after you've wasted an absurd amount of energy. Even worse, you might not realize that a contact is of value because you haven't defined your intent for yourself or the other person.

The Networlding Support Exchange Model

We refer to networking connections as flimsy because they lack support. In networking, people are bound together because one person needs another to do a deal or create a sale. One particular situation binds them together, and as soon as this situation disintegrates or disappears, there's nothing left to hold the relationship together. Networlders, in contrast, are connected by the ascending levels of support shown in the support exchange model. (See Figure 1.1.)

The model illustrates the hierarchy of the development of relationships, which evolves from a conscious communication exchange process with a select group of people.

Figure 1.1. The Networlding Support Exchange Model.

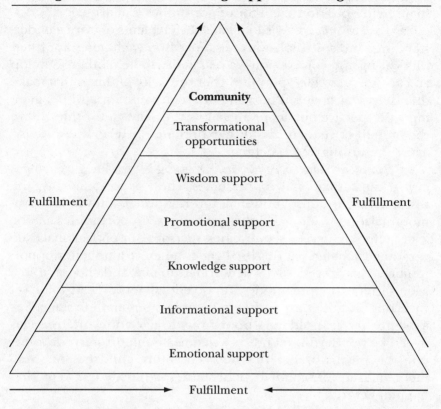

- *Emotional support.* This is the part of consciousness that involves feelings. Our feelings about others serve as the foundation for our relationships. The focus of exchanging emotional support with another is to create rapport, a relationship of mutual trust and affinity.
- *Informational support.* Information is a combination of messages. Once initial rapport is built, we then feel comfortable to share information of value.
- *Knowledge support.* Here, we add the element of experience. By sharing our personal experiences and those of others we have heard about, we add additional value to our exchanges with others.
- *Promotional support.* As we continue to build rapport, we naturally share with others the strengths of those whom we value. We

raise our Networlding partners' awareness of others, and in doing so we better position them for opportunities that arise.

• *Wisdom support.* Wisdom adds the elements of clarity, understanding, and spiritual awareness. Wisdom exchanges are filled with caring and compassion—a real desire to help others develop and achieve their life's purpose. There are a lot of things that make themselves clear only after you have seen them for a while, gaining a perspective not achievable any other way. Networlders have the benefit of years of rich life experiences. Here, there is also active mentoring and coaching.

• *Transformational opportunities.* Ongoing Networlding exchanges evolve transformational opportunities. These opportunities are the result of continuous emotional, informational, knowledge, promotional, and wisdom support exchanges. Opportunities can be leads; referrals; new jobs; or business, personal, or professional. Networlding exchanges at this level generate more and better opportunities. This process allows networlders to pick and choose from a wide variety of opportunities. It also allows networlders to direct their opportunities according to their passions and life stage. For a twenty-five-year-old, an opportunity to live and work overseas would be wonderful, yet not as welcome an opportunity for someone, say, in his or her thirties with young children. At some moment, transformational opportunities are created that couldn't happen before.

• *Community.* This level of support results from a series of exchanges. There is a ripple effect that occurs as each Networlding partner shares the benefits of various forms of support with others in his or her community, support that is potentially shared with others, and so on and so forth. As multiple Networlding exchanges make a difference in the networlder's life, they continue to make a difference in the lives of others.

• *Fulfillment.* A deep, personal sense of satisfaction comes from finding your purpose, and then using that purpose to fulfill your destiny and create your legacy. Throughout the Networlding process, networlders receive fulfillment from exchanges individually, and even greater satisfaction from the awareness that they are making a difference in the lives of others. Fulfillment is both internal (for example, self-satisfaction) and external (as with larger salaries or business opportunities).

Let's look at an example. Jean Nidetch, president of multimillion-dollar Weight Watchers International, created a successful dieting empire by actively engaging in each of these types of meaningful exchanges with friends and customers alike. Because Nidetch provided the emotional and informational support her customers needed to be successful in losing weight, her customers rewarded her with promotional support, leads, and referrals that resulted in tremendous sales and profits.

These types of support exchanges make it infinitely easier to develop opportunities with others. In networking, one or both networkers shy away from opportunity development because they feel that they're imposing or being imposed on. Networking frequently produces win-lose situations rather than win-win situations, and thus reluctance to explore opportunities. People know they're using others or being used.

When networking partners manage to work on an opportunity together, it is almost always a "directed" opportunity. In other words, one of the people directs the other based on what he or she wants to accomplish. Although Networlding may also involve directed opportunities, the direction is based on mutual interest and intent. It also offers the possibility of free-flowing opportunities. As you begin to exchange information, ideas, and experiences with others in your circle, new needs and opportunities may begin to surface that lead to the development of these free-flowing opportunities. Your combined intention and attention shift to brainstorming answers collectively. Ultimately, this "circle brainstorming" offers actionable solutions and real opportunities.

How Do You Rate as a Networlder?

Are you a networlder? Some people naturally practice Networlding, but most of us have to work at it. Networking has been the norm for a long time, and it has probably colored your view of finding and maintaining relationships. Although you may believe in Networlding principles, you may have difficulty putting those principles to work for you.

A Web site focusing on women's lifestyles titled *ivillage.com* conducted a survey about networking over the Internet. Eleven hundred women and men working in various industries were involved.

Sixty-seven percent of those responding indicated that forming relationships and using those connections to get ahead were critical for their success. They also stated that they did not know how to leverage their relationships in meaningful ways. Still others were apprehensive about pursuing connections to develop opportunities—especially the one-sided networking type—or concerned that improperly using this strategy could mean professional or social suicide.

We've found that there is a great deal of confusion and concern about how to make and maintain connections. People are apprehensive not only about the actual process but how good they are at it. When we introduce Networlding to people during workshops, lectures, and other forums, they're often not sure if they're pursuing relationships and opportunities in an intentional, values-driven way.

The Networlding Quiz

So are you a networlder, a networker, or neither? Take the Networlding quiz shown in Exhibit 1.1 to discover what your Networlding IQ really is and what it could become. This quiz is based on the beliefs, strategies, and behaviors of expert networlders from a variety of industries and professional disciplines. By completing it you will be able to compare your ideas and skills with those of the experts, giving you insight into how you might change your approach.

Answer each of the questions in this quiz. Indicate how often you practice the behaviors listed using numbers 1 to 5 as follows: (1) never, (2) seldom, (3) occasionally, (4) often, or (5) always. Total your score once you have completed the quiz. This is your Networlding IQ. To know how you rank as a networlder, compare your score with those shown at the end of the exercise. The section following the quiz will give you a better understanding of just what your score means.

Interpreting Your Networlding IQ

If your score reveals you to be a novice or a networker, don't be alarmed. It's relatively rare to encounter a natural networlder; these are learned rather than inherent behaviors. Still, if you want

Exhibit 1.1. The Networlding Quiz.

	Always (5)	Often (4)	Occasionally (3)	Seldom (2)	Never (1)
I believe it is important to make a difference.	✓				
I believe that anything is possible.					
I believe that I am guided by strong inner beliefs, intent, or principles.	✓				
I believe that I can get anything done through others.					
I believe that people are my most creative resource.					
I share my goals with others.					
I build-nurture relationships with those who can help me achieve my goals.	✓				
I limit relationships with selfish individuals and those that don't help me realize my goals.					
I respect the creative process and am results- or outcome-focused.					
I believe that Networlding-networking shortens the time to get things done.					
I assume that Networlding-networking is a balanced process of giving and receiving.					
I believe that Networlding-networking can provide all needed resources to reach my goals.	✓				
When Networlding-networking, I ask for what I want.					
When Networlding-networking, I discover others' interests and needs.					
When Networlding-networking, I expect to discover or create new opportunities.					
I network-network with influential people who can make things happen.					
I offer emotional, informational, and other support to my networld-network partners.					
I respond quickly to the requests and needs of my networld-network partners.					
I measure the results of my Networlding-networking efforts.					

Note on scoring: 20–44: novice; 45–64: networker; 65–84: strategic networlder; 85–100: Networlding expert.

to lead a fulfilling, successful life in our interconnected world, you're going to need to move from simple networking to expert Networlding. As the quiz suggests, expert networlders have mastered the exchange of all types of support and drive continuous opportunities through collaboration. To achieve this mastery, you must pass through four levels: novice, networker, strategic networlder, and Networlding expert. The how-tos of advancing through these levels are presented in later chapters, but the basic explanations for each level are discussed as follows.

Novice (Score: 20–44)

If you scored from 20 to 44 points on the quiz, you are an entry-level networker or novice. You are likely to have cultivated a baseline network of friends and family members. You may also participate in professional, political, or community organizations but are unlikely to play a leading role in the management of them or their major events. Perhaps you have thought about your intent and the goals necessary to achieve it. It may be that you've considered your goals, beliefs, and values and the need to find and form compatible relationships. What you haven't done is share these thoughts with others in ways that create meaningful opportunities.

You're reluctant to do so because you feel uncomfortable using connections to get what you want or engaging in traditional "meeting-and-greeting" behaviors. Fear of rejection or doubt that you have anything valuable to offer others may be keeping you in the novice category.

The good news is that you can probably turn at least some of your contacts into meaningful collaborative relationships. The opportunities and support that Networlding offers is not as far away as you might think. As you'll discover, a relatively simple shift in attitude and behaviors will have you Networlding in no time.

Networker (Score: 45–64)

You are a true networker, having scored 45 to 64 points on the quiz. You are likely to have expanded beyond your circle of family, friends, and colleagues to include individuals from industry associations and important local and community organizations. You recognize influential people—known as influencers—and make every effort to meet with them. You are likely to pass out cards and contact information to a broad array of potential influencers and to follow up with them. Consequently, you have a large card file or computerized directory of names and contacts.

Yet despite your ability to meet and greet, you are not generating the quality of relationships or the type of opportunities you are interested in pursuing. Part of the problem may be that all those names you've accumulated do not really represent relationships; those people may not remember you when you get around to calling them, or you may be fuzzy about who they are. Or you establish a superficial relationship, exchanging information and some support, but the trust and shared goals aren't there for opportunities to develop. By learning to focus your efforts on developing relationships that are based on valuable exchanges, you can begin to experience the naturally beneficial opportunities that Networlding provides.

Strategic Networlder (Score: 65–84)

As a strategic networlder with a score of 65 to 84 points, you have moved well beyond traditional networking and entered the realm of Networlding. You now do the following:

- Target and qualify those with whom you spend your time based on your goals, values, and beliefs
- Share your intent with those in your circle and understand theirs
- Grow your important target contacts into meaningful relationships
- Exchange different types of support with others
- Schedule meetings and regularly follow up with referral sources
- Leverage your relationships to develop opportunities for yourself and others

You are instinctively doing the right things. Now you will have the chance to broaden your Networlding skills into a systematic approach for even greater success.

Networlding Expert (Score: 85–100)

If you are a Networlding expert, you are a top-level networlder because you do this:

- Broaden your Networlding circles to include divergent members—people who represent a broad spectrum of interests and skills and who provide you with access to more varied and significant opportunities
- Exchange support on all levels
- Acquire whatever resources you lack through others
- Interact with influential individuals who can help you reach your goals through mutually beneficial opportunities
- Engage in cross-level Networlding to form personal strategic alliances, to collaborate on projects, and to develop new opportunities with others

In the words of Zig Zigler, the highly successful salesman and motivational speaker, you are not only doing the right things but doing things right. You will now learn to refresh, refine, and further extend your Networlding skills and processes to achieve even greater fulfillment.

Increasing Your Networlding IQ

The four rating categories are provided to give you a sense of where you are on the relationship-building to opportunity-creating continuum; they are not absolutes. For instance, Networlding experts can still improve their Networlding ability. Networking novices can very quickly transition into Networlding. Some strategic networlders are much further along in their development than others in the same grouping. In the following chapters, we're not going to dwell on these categories; we will only mention them as guideposts along the way. Your goal should not be to achieve expert status as much as to keep improving on the skills, behaviors, and mind-set that high-level Networlding represents. Continuous improvement, therefore, is what we're going to stress.

People who continuously improve or move quickly along the continuum are those who visualize their networld, establish connections with bridgers, create inner and outer circles to "hold" their Networlding relationships, identify and include influencers, and maximize their connectivity. Let's examine each of these Networlding facilitators and how they might help you become a networlder.

Visualize Your Networld

Your networld is a series of organic connections between yourself, people with resources, and your opportunities. Two familiar images may serve to represent these connections: a bull's-eye with you at its center, with your relationships forming the surrounding concentric circles; and an orchestra that produces incredible music with you as the conductor. The best image, however, is a living organism. This is because Networlding is an ongoing process of relationship building, exchange, and opportunity creation. Your networld transforms and evolves with your intent and that of your networld members. Collectively you give birth to many mutually beneficial opportunities as you move toward the achievement of your goals.

To form your own more personalized picture of a networld, imagine yourself at the center of a dynamic, functioning organism. You are connected to many specialized cells that work together to accomplish the organism's various goals, like eating, breathing, and so on. These cells work collectively according to what appears to be an invisible directive. They are efficient and productive, and each cell benefits from the actions undertaken. As the organism grows, it changes form, learns new things, and gains new experiences. It adds, expels, and replaces cells. Each cell has a dynamic relationship to the whole, growing and expiring throughout the life of the organism. Finally, the organism combines with another organism to realize its greatest accomplishment: reproduction or the creation of a new life.

In your networld, you are surrounded by cells—those in your primary, secondary, and tertiary relationship circles. Like specialized cells, each of these people serve unique functions. Some have tremendous influence and are regular, active partners with you; others lend occasional support. This is a dynamic rather than a static universe you've created. You're bringing in and moving out people continuously based on evolving goals.

Think about having access to this diverse group of people. Imagine a steady stream of opportunities flowing by you and being able to access whatever resources you need to take advantage of these opportunities. Furthermore, visualize the people in this dynamic universe as being individuals you implicitly like, trust, and respect. They are not in the universe for the money or any other reason but because they are compatible with you on many levels.

If you can visualize yourself as part of this networld—if this system strikes you as something that you want to create—then you're starting off on the right foot. You want to shift your frame of reference from a flat, static series of contacts to an evolving, multi-level group of connections. Just shifting your thinking about the types of relationships you can develop will help you see the Net-worlding possibilities. If you have doubts about whether such a networld is possible—especially if you're skeptical about your own ability to establish the right relationships—then consider this: you are closer to your future networld partners than you think.

Establish Connections with Bridgers

In John Guare's play *Six Degrees of Separation,* Ouisa, one of the lead characters, explains the people-connection phenomenon as follows: "I read somewhere that everybody on this planet is separated by only six other people. Six degrees of separation. Between us and everybody else on this planet. The President of the United States. A gondolier in Venice. How every person is a new door, opening up into other worlds. Six degrees of separation between me and everyone else on this planet." (Guare, 1990, p. 81).

Indeed, noted scholars have studied the "people puzzle," or the random connections between individuals, since the 1960s. Yale sociologist Sam Milgram's study of a group of midwesterners' relationships to strangers on the East Coast and mathematicians Steven Strogatz and Duncan Watts's writings on the relationships between working actors all conclude that people can connect with any individual in only a few steps using well-placed intermediaries. We call these intermediaries *bridgers.* They are individuals who bring together people from different groups to develop new opportunities. Bridgers can be just about anyone, from well-placed people in organizations who connect across departmental boundaries to family members, neighbors, friends, and PTA members.

Because of the relationships bridgers have cultivated in different areas of their lives, they are invaluable resources in helping you connect with others to achieve your goals. Bridgers may not provide you directly with opportunities or even offer you support, but what they will do is link you to others who will become your Net-worlding partners. They serve an important "middleman" function because both you and the person they help you link up with trust the bridger. This trust makes it easier to explore and establish a relationship with a stranger.

For example, Jose, a local entrepreneur, is an extraordinary bridger. He knows people from large and small businesses, community organizations, and government agencies. Jose often connects people from his various groups, and these connections catalyze opportunities. He has a matchmaker's instinct, an ability to see many of the compatible qualities we've discussed. Jose benefits in many ways from the connections he helps establish; he receives a great deal of return business from the grateful friends and associates he brings together. Though he may not be in the networld proper, he exists on its periphery and serves a valuable function.

If you can find bridgers in your personal and professional life, they can quickly eliminate whatever degrees of separation exist between you and the people who will make tremendous Networlding partners. Bridgers are easily identifiable; they're the ones who seem to know everyone, have a knack for anticipating who will work well together, and relish the chance to make the introductions.

Create Inner and Outer Circles

As we've already suggested, you will need different circles of people surrounding you in your networld. This is because all relationships are not the same, and networlders learn that if they organize their relationships according to type (frequency of contact, level of exchange, type of opportunities developed, and so on), they can enjoy much more productive relationships. Networkers tend to have disorganized, undifferentiated relationships, and this prevents them from focusing their energy on the right people at the right time.

Organizing and differentiating for networlders means dividing relationships into primary, secondary, and tertiary circles, as illustrated in Figure 1.2. The primary circle is made up of people with whom you have frequent contact and exchanges of support, and they're the ones who are most closely aligned with your goals and values. This primary group usually consists of three to ten influential individuals with whom you develop opportunities. In this primary circle, the relationships are proactive. People know each other well and share beliefs and objectives, enabling them to anticipate the needs of others in the circle. This means that you're not always calling someone for help, but there is a balance of asking for and giving help.

Jackie is a member of Leon's primary circle. After working closely with Leon, a marketing manager in his mid-thirties who has an engineering background, Jackie was truly impressed with his motivation and talent. Because she knew that Leon wanted to be a general manger, she recommended him for operating assignments both inside and outside of her company. As a result of her recommendations, he received an opportunity to manage an international joint venture and later to manage a large, growing telecommunications operation. In turn, Jackie received admiration and gratitude from both Leon and his employer. As his influence grew, Leon reciprocated by referring Jackie to the president of his company to fill a senior management role that he knew she

Figure 1.2. Building Strong Circles.

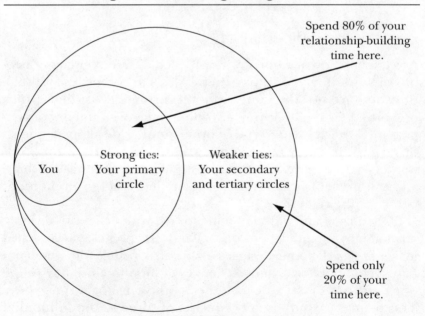

would be interested in and qualified to do. In addition, Jackie and Leon are working on an idea for a new business that represents a mutual opportunity.

Invariably, the interactions between people in primary circles lead to supplementary relationships. Through the inner circle of your networld, you meet people who form the outer or secondary and tertiary circles. Usually, someone in your primary circle refers you to an individual who becomes part of your outer circles. For example, the president of Leon's company became part of Jackie's secondary circle. Your secondary circle can be several times the size of your primary one because the need for regular contact and support isn't as great. Therefore, you don't have to expend the same amount of time and emotional energy as you do in your primary circle.

Secondary circles are valuable because they help you develop greater information, broader perspectives, and enhanced influence. In most instances, secondary circles are more diverse than primary ones and can provide a greater range of ideas, information, and referrals. Tertiary circles are formed from the "spillover" from secondary circles. The tertiary circles consist of the individuals you see the least often but who can deliver—if infrequently—useful facts, ideas, and other types of support.

The bonds that you form with people in these various circles hold them together. It is unrealistic to expect that you'll have equally strong bonds with each person in each circle. Nor is that necessary. Weak bonds may be fine, especially if your relationship with someone in a tertiary circle is built on an information exchange. As much as possible, however, you should strive to transition weak bonds into stronger ones. By doing so, you increase the chances of having successful Networlding relationships and opportunities. Bonds built on trust produce the most valuable and sensitive insights, information, and opportunities. After all, you are likely to invite someone to participate with you in a great business opportunity only if you trust and respect the person.

Because it's impossible to form strong bonds with everyone, you should concentrate on forming your strongest bonds with people in your primary circle; they're the ones with whom you have the most in common and the most contact. Beyond that, focus on creating exceptionally deep and meaningful relationships with the people we refer to as *influencers*.

Identify and Include Influencers

In the old business scenario, influential individuals used to be called the "powerful" people. Using power, however, is no longer the way things get done in our world. Too often, powerful people make things happen in the short term at the expense of long-term results, and they alienate so many people that they lose others' loyalty, enthusiasm, and initiative.

Influencers, in contrast, may have "position power" based on their titles or jobs but they don't issue orders to get things done. Instead, they use their knowledge, skills, experience, reputation, resources, and connections to make things happen. Although influencers might be CEOs or people who occupy high-level positions, they may also be just about anyone—opinion-making journalists, trend-setting industry leaders, community activists, inventors, and so on. It all depends on what your goals are and if a given individual is able to influence others to help you achieve these goals.

Consider Jim, who had the good fortune of finding a great influencer during a sales call. After striking up a conversation with the receptionist at one of his customers, Jim asked her who she knew well at the company. The receptionist surprised Jim by saying that she was close with the CEO because she and her husband often went antiques shopping with the CEO and her husband. Jim's decision to create a strong bond with this receptionist wasn't mercenary. He didn't particularly want her to put in a good word with the CEO or intervene on his behalf in any way. But after talking with her, Jim realized that she knew more about the business than anyone he had ever met. It was no wonder that she was friendly with the CEO as well as a number of other people in the industry. Her insights into customer service problems were incredibly perceptive, and she was well aware of the techniques being used to try and solve these problems. This receptionist was an unlikely influencer because of her job, but she was an influencer nonetheless. She shared her insights with Jim, and he was able to develop a program that eventually brought him an enormous amount of business.

Influencers are often natural networlders, if not in name then in deed. They are well known and often well respected in their sphere of influence (this receptionist had the respect of everyone, and the company's top executives frequently shared ideas with her). They often support or mentor others.

Christine is an influencer who built her career as a successful consultant for Fortune 500 firms. Recently, she had a rare opportunity to establish an office in Europe. She located her office in London and joined the city's chamber of commerce. She worked on several chamber committees focused on policy issues, volunteering her consulting services to support the efforts of small businesses in London. Because of her genuine concern and efforts for small businesses and chamber policies, Christine grew both her influence and her networld in the London business community. And it paid off for her when she was elected as the first woman chair of London's chamber of commerce.

Maximize Your Connectivity

We would be remiss if we failed to discuss electronic communications as a Networlding facilitator. There is still no substitute for connecting in person to build rapport or establish an emotional link. In the most recent DDB Needham lifestyle study, the percentages for going out and interacting with others at movies, sporting events, and casinos increased 10 percent to 19 percent over the same activities in 1988. In a Roper study, face-to-face financial transactions were seen to be preferred three to eight times over telephone or on-line transactions.

But ironically, it is becoming more difficult for us to connect and have effective personal and social interactions. Growing time pressures mean we participate less in clubs, community projects, and entertaining in our homes. Some of us even believe that we are losing our ability to talk and socialize effectively with others (DDB Needham Emotional Needs Study).

Given this situation, we've found that electronic communications can enhance our ability to connect with others. Networlders rely on e-mail and the Internet as both relationship-building and maintenance tools. Although they should not be a substitute for face-to-face encounters, they are a valuable supplement. Networlders often target specific user groups. They use a variety of sources to identify the individuals with whom to connect, including on-line mailing lists,

Web sites, news groups, and more. Networlders use e-mail and Internet to exchange all types of information, ideas, and even emotional support. People can initiate relationships in chat rooms that blossom into "real world" partnerships; an electronic exchange can lead to a face-to-face meeting. Conversely, relationships that begin in the real world can deepen through electronic dialogues.

Electronic communication often accelerates relationship-building for many networlders, moving them quickly through the following four relationship stages: *lack of awareness* (that is, they are complete strangers); *awareness* (knowledge of the other is one-sided); *mutual awareness* (two parties have knowledge of each other but have not met); and contact or *acquaintance* (two parties meet or exchange e-mail). Sociologist Linton Freeman analyzed the impact of electronic communication on relationship building. Measuring the degree and speed of social scientists moving through the four stages of building relationships, he found that none of the control group, which did not have e-mail or conferencing tools, moved through all four stages within the seven-month study period. In contrast, over 30 percent of the group with electronic communications tools moved into the third phase of mutual awareness quickly and none in this group remained in the first phase by the end of the study. Indeed, Valdis Krebs, a consultant on social networks and organizational behavior, concludes that on-line connectivity may provide social networks that are an order of magnitude larger and stronger than what we have commonly experienced.

So don't avoid electronic communication because you feel it is superficial or vastly inferior to personal communication. Like anything else, it can be misused or abused, and we wouldn't recommend spending all or most of your time on Internet relationships. However, you should explore different Web sites, news groups, user groups, and knowledge circles, initiating relationships and strengthening existing ones. For example, Six Degrees, located at www.sixdegrees.com, is one of the foremost connection Web sites. Six Degrees enables users to connect with thousands of individuals who have interests similar to theirs. Similarly, Participate.com supports the development of premier knowledge circles in companies and across industries. There is even a networlding.com Web site to provide ongoing information, opportunities, and connections among socially conscious networlders.

Now That You Know What Networlding Is, What Should You Do?

The actual practice of Networlding may seem intimidating. After all, it's one thing to work a room, it's something else entirely to establish primary circles, identify influencers, and build mutually rewarding relationships that lead to opportunities. We want to assure you, however, that Networlding is something that anyone can do. Although it requires a bit of thought and effort, people gain proficiency at it relatively quickly.

One of the things that will help you get started is knowing the rules. Unlike networking, there is a science as well as an art to this relationship-building and opportunity-creating process. In the next chapter, we will look at the specific rules that will govern your Networlding behaviors, help you meet the people who you need to meet, and create your opportunities.

◯ CHAPTER TWO

Networlding Golden Rules

Networlding works because its fundamental rules fit with the new principles for success in our interconnected world. Networlding recognizes the importance of collaboration over isolation, of information over capital, of diversity over uniformity, of values over amorality, of influence over power. The golden rules of Networlding describe how you should treat others and how you should expect to be treated. They explain how your networld should work. Collectively, they represent the "golden thread" that connects successful Networlding relationships and opportunities.

To networld successfully, you need to become familiar with these rules. There are many ways to form and maintain relationships, and it's easy to fall back on old behaviors, bad habits, and networking advice. These rules will keep you focused on Networlding relationships and opportunities, and guide what you do and say to achieve them.

Rule One: Make the Connection

First, realize that you are connected to everyone and everything. Many people don't make those phone calls, contact other people electronically, send letters, introduce themselves at conferences, or arrange meetings because they don't realize how close they are to the people who will be most important to them. Through your work, family, friends, and community, you have far more connections than you may realize.

Thus, you need to see connections where they don't seem to exist. This "seeing" will provide you with the impetus to act. Once you realize that not only people but information, ideas, emotional support, referrals, and opportunities are links on the chain—and that you're only a link or two away from all these things—then you're much more likely to initiate relationships. Remember, too, that Networlding provides you with tools to make connections. Bridgers extend the reach of your connections, and influencers can affect people in a way that they bring you what you require. The Internet, too, accelerates the speed with which you make connections and provides you with another way to develop and deepen relationships.

Networlders connect with the right people because they have the confidence to take the initiative. Part of the confidence and initiative flows from the realization that they already possess everything, or can gain access to anything, they need to accomplish their goals. Making connections is much easier once you acknowledge that this process isn't a long shot; valuable experiences, resources, and opportunities are inevitable if you establish and grow your networld.

Rule Two: Think and Link

Awareness and intention are crucial for networlders. You need to be alert to the possibility of a connection in every situation. Because you know you are connected to everyone and everything you need—see Rule One—you don't have to become a frenzied networker, constantly passing out your business cards. What you do have to do is think all the time about potential linkages when you're with people you know as well as with new people.

The paradox of Networlding is that as close as your connections are, they often aren't immediately apparent. You have to develop a thought process that reflexively searches for invisible connections. Good networlders have an instinct about this invisible linkage. After a brief meeting, they sense if someone has the potential to be in one their circles.

This ability comes with experience, but it also comes with a willingness to move past fears and ego in order to think about everyone as a potential Networlding partner. You can also recognize hidden linkages if you clarify your intent—your goals, values, and needs. By verbally identifying your intent, you may see what formerly was invisible. People respond to your intent in ways that help you see what their goals, values, and needs are. Suddenly, an individual who seemed irrelevant to your purpose becomes very important to what you hope to achieve.

The concept of linkages or connections is a broad one, and some of the connections you make may lie dormant for weeks or even months after you make them. Others, however, are "hot." Hot links simply mean that a person is actively willing and able to provide you with resources and opportunities; he or she also will proactively put you in touch with other hot links he or she knows. You can ignite a hot link if you focus on people you meet as well as communicate your intent.

Vanessa, a successful corporate saleswoman and the mother of two young children, wanted to find a stimulating and flexible career that allowed her more time with her children. Vanessa mentioned her intention to John, a friend who wanted to start a software firm, thinking she could offer her selling skills to help him grow the business. They decided to form a partnership and entered the software business. As sales grew, they began to look for other ways in which they could collaborate for even greater success. John connected Vanessa with a professional speakers' group he had worked with. She went on several speaking engagements for him, touting the capabilities of the software firm. Because she gave these speeches, Vanessa was able to streamline the selling process and reduce the number of sales calls she made. Consequently, she gained more flexibility and free time. John gained broader awareness for his software business, and they both gained more potential customers and income. By realizing and activating the inherent connections between their networlds and their goals, Vanessa and John were able to create several good opportunities for each other aligned with their intent.

Both Vanessa and John also realized the importance of thinking and linking. They didn't think of each other only as friends but saw beyond the friendship to the connective power of the relationship. Then they actively began linking and exploring mutual opportunities.

Rule Three: Expand Your Connections

Networlders are open to new possibilities. They are always increasing their skills, knowledge, and experiences because they're receptive to taking advantage of all the new things being offered them. There is a constant flow of information, experiences, and ideas along networld lines, and you must find what's relevant to your goals and move with them in new directions. In effect, you're expanding your networld by pursuing your goals, embracing new experiences, and developing new skills. You will naturally connect to a larger set of people and opportunities when you do this.

As you begin to move expertly through your networld, you will become aware of your own flexibility. You will realize that you have many and varied resources with which to create new opportunities. You may be a traditional marketer who finds an opportunity in Internet marketing. You may be a businessperson who is exposed to the world of nonprofit organizations. Wherever your connections take you, don't resist. Networlders have more options than others because they don't impose strict boundaries on who they are or what they do.

Rachelle, an MBA with a strong track record in marketing, had a career dilemma. She had recently been promoted into a job that was now going to be based in another city. If she took the opportunity, her husband would have to find a new job, her children would have to start over in a new school, the family would have to move out of their newly built home, and they would have to reestablish themselves in a different community. Although she really enjoyed her job, Rachelle dreaded the move. She decided to explore her connections, and she found a link between her business and social networld.

Gordon was part of Rachelle's secondary Networlding circle, but his area of expertise was training. In the past Rachelle hadn't thought their goals dovetailed. Still, Gordon was a good friend and the two provided a good deal of emotional support for each other. Faced with this career dilemma, however, Rachelle consciously looked at all her connections in a more open-minded way. As a result, she and Gordon had a number of discussions about the training field. Shortly thereafter, Gordon was given an assignment to develop a new team focusing on expert marketing performance training. Rachelle had learned a lot about training from him, and she liked what she had learned. Just as important, her marketing expertise would be a valuable addition to his team. In the end, Rachelle interviewed for the job and got it. After meeting with consultants and educators, she found she brought new practical insights and approaches to marketing training. She had a networld of strong marketers to benchmark for best practices to teach new marketing managers. She knew how marketers used research in their decision making, and she successfully incorporated research modules into the training program. She not only avoided having to move but also expanded her networld in an important way. Rachelle moved Gordon into her primary circle and eventually added a number of other people whom she never would have met if she had remained in her traditional marketing niche. In doing so, Rachelle also expanded her career opportunities.

Rule Four: Make Both Your Redundant and Divergent Connections Count

Redundant connections are relationships of the same or similar type. Maria, a very successful manager in the insurance industry, had a strong primary circle in her company and a vast secondary circle in her industry. But as people moved from company to company, the two circles began to overlap. As colleagues met other insurance colleagues who met other colleagues, the dividing lines between the two groups blurred. Everyone knew everyone else. Although this led to great camaraderie, it prevented Maria from achieving the diversity networlders require.

Networkers often suffer from redundant connections. They may know a lot of people, but they are all the same sort of people (the same industry, the same company, the same location, and so on). There's the illusion of diversity because of the size of the network, but it's not the reality. Networks are often just big, homogeneous clusters. As a result, little new or outside information or resources come into the networks and fewer new opportunities are realized. Mel is another victim of this phenomenon. He had been out of work for a year despite his constant networking with just about everyone he knew in his industry. Because each contact pointed to another contact in the same industry and because his industry was downsizing, no one knew of any good job opportunities for Mel.

Divergent connections involve a much more diverse group of people. These connections usually lead in new and unfamiliar directions, exposing networlders to new experiences, ideas, and so on. By providing new information and access to more resources, these divergent connections accelerate the process. The rule, therefore, is to make sure you're tapping into as diverse a group as possible. This doesn't mean that you should ignore redundant connections but rather that you should widen the circle to include a divergent mix.

Sometimes this can be amazingly easy to do. Let's get back to Mel's story. After fruitlessly searching for a new job in his industry for a year, he mentioned his situation to one of the fathers he knew from his son's Little League team, a man Mel liked and had always felt was a kindred spirit. That man suggested that Mel speak to one of the managers at his firm, who needed someone to help create a new department. Mel soon found himself with a new career in a growing industry. By moving from his homogeneous professional connections to his more diverse personal connections, Mel was able to tap into a new career opportunity.

Divergent connections should also include people who are at different position levels than you are. Shared goals, values, and beliefs can help you transcend whatever barriers keep you from meaningful interactions with CEOs and other top executives. We don't mean that you can just approach the head of an organization, introduce yourself, and expect a Networlding relationship to follow. Our point is that you should attempt this connection if you believe there is potential for a relationship. Communicating your intent quickly and clearly can attract the attention of someone in a powerful position.

For instance, Naomi, a Japanese exchange student who worked in an American manufacturing plant, heard through the office grapevine that an important Japanese customer was coming to visit the factory. She had heard a great deal about him and admired his ideas and accomplishments, and she believed that, despite the gap in their positions, they thought alike and had the same business philosophies.

On the day of the visit, Naomi dressed in her best suit and waited patiently until the entourage of company officials and the Japanese customer entered her work area in the factory. Nervous but determined, she approached the customer. Knowing that she risked being fired by her company, she welcomed him in Japanese and explained her job. The visitor was surprised but impressed, and he gave her his card.

When she went to Japan for the holidays, she arranged a meeting with the customer, during which she promised to address any issues he might have right at the factory-floor level. He was again impressed and brought Naomi to her senior management's attention. When she later identified a quality problem that would have caused the products to be rejected by the Japanese customer, management promoted her to the position of quality inspector. So began Naomi's rise in the corporation, where she is now an executive.

Rule Five: Grow and Nurture Your Relationships

Like fruit-bearing trees, networlds yield the sweetest opportunities when the relationships between its members have taken root and grown strong and their fruit has ripened. It's not "just business." Your relationships with people—especially those in your primary circle—must involve common intent, trust, and values; a mutual exchange of ideas, resources, and emotional support; and a commitment to pursue opportunities together. These sorts of relationships don't happen overnight or without considerable effort.

Keep this rule in mind so you don't become frustrated as you're developing your networld. Networlds, like relationships, take time. If you maintain your focus on nurturing relationships, both you and your Networlding partner will eventually reap the benefits. Though it might not seem so at the time, you're both establishing a foundation that will make it much easier to capitalize on an opportunity when the situation is right. Because you know each other so well, trust each other, and are familiar with each other's strengths, you can move with speed and synergy.

Joyce's friend Linda dreamed of becoming an international businessperson. Joyce and Linda had met in business school. They liked each other and kept in touch over the years. They provided useful information, shared personal successes and disappointments, and generally supported each other. Thanks to these exchanges, they both experienced small rewards over the years. But it was nearly fifteen years after the friendship began that Joyce, by now a senior executive at a Fortune 500 company, learned that her organization was having great difficulty in restructuring a recently acquired European company. The company needed someone who had both broad-based financial and investment skills and sensitivity to people issues. There weren't many such people around, and it was fortuitous that one of Joyce's closest friends—Linda—fit this description. Although Linda had a successful consulting practice, she had never had an international opportunity like this before. Joyce arranged for Linda to spearhead the project as a consultant and then move onto the selection committee that would choose the new CEO. The assignment—successfully completed by Linda and her group—moved her to a higher level as an international consultant. Joyce too benefited, because she appeared to be a genius by suggesting the company go the consultant route: the restructuring was completed and profitable far more quickly than if the company had searched for a CEO right from the start as originally planned. If Joyce and Linda hadn't grown and nurtured their relationship over the years, Joyce would never have had the confidence to recommend Linda for the assignment.

Rule Six: Make Your Exchanges Meaningful

Networlding opportunities are catalyzed by a meaningful exchange between people. Meaningful exchanges not only cement relationships but also often trigger ideas, confidence, and initiative that result in a mutually beneficial opportunity. Although exchanges come in many different forms—emotional support, informational support, promotional support, and so on—networlders are willing to take the risks such exchanges demand. Sometimes the risk is emotional; you need to be open and honest and may risk offending your Networlding partner. Sometimes the risk involves trust; you're revealing a piece of information that could get you in trouble if others found out you had disclosed it. But taking this risk and exchanging something meaningful creates all sorts of sparks. With strong emotional support or precious new data, you can move forward with confidence and knowledge.

Information is becoming an especially meaningful exchange in our interconnected world. The organizations that know the most do the best. The Internet has made information exchanges easier and faster, and it has made everyone aware of the importance of obtaining the right data at the right time. Things are changing so quickly that if your information is only a little outdated, it's worthless. Networlders don't hoard information. Instead, they give it freely, knowing that they'll receive equally valuable information in return. Networlders operate with their eyes open. They possess cutting-edge knowledge that can help them move faster than others and in the right direction.

We should add that *meaningful* is a key word in exchanges, whether they involve information or the other areas we've discussed. Trivial or mundane exchanges don't count. Networkers often exchange gossip rather than substantive ideas; they are involved in relatively meaningless chatter. Networlders put their heart and soul into their exchanges; they don't hold back and they don't limit themselves to the superficial and inconsequential.

Rule Seven: Collaborate for Success

This may seem like an obvious point until you realize that *collaborate* is a word that is open to interpretation. Networkers often collaborate briefly, selfishly, and superficially. Others collaborate sincerely but without a sense of structure or shared goals. We see collaboration as a highly focused process, one that requires two minds working together with a single intent. In our view, collaboration is synergistic and value-driven. Because of the trust, compatible beliefs, and shared goals among networlders, collaborations are more intense and more productive. There's none of the divisiveness and suspicion that marks many collaborative efforts.

From a Networlding perspective, collaborations also possess an exponential force. Although they begin between two people, other networlders are often brought into the mix. The collaborative goal orbits around a primary circle, gaining strength from the contributions of others. People are open and honest. Thus, sometimes a collaborative project may not make it to the opportunity stage because fatal flaws are uncovered. But even this scenario results in further collaborations. As disappointed as people are if a project doesn't work out, they are energized by the Networlding collaborative dynamic and eager to try again.

However, many Networlding collaborations produce wonderful new ideas, careers, businesses, products, and services because of their exponential power. True collaboration increases the chances of success because more and better things emerge from these efforts. Because networlders invite others to participate in their collaborations, the invitation usually results in a chain reaction of additional collaborations: Joe and Mary work together on an idea, Mary tells Cindy, Cindy brings in Tom to help, Tom contacts Mark, and on and on it goes.

Here's a story that gives a sense of how an initial idea can blossom through collaborative invitation. When a young computer science student named Linus Torvalds put his Linux version of the UNIX operating system on the Internet in 1991, it was not the best operating system ever created. But in less than three years and with contributions from thousands of software engineers and techie types around the world, the Linux operating system was touted as the best.

The UNIX operating system is used in large computers in business and academic organizations. Torvalds developed the basic software code for his Linux version and then encouraged others to debug, modify, and improve his original code over the Internet. As the word spread throughout the software community, more and more of them added their insights, creating a highly innovative operating system. They did so employing a new approach that required far less time and money than traditional software development, and that created greater value for users.

Torvalds's networld may not exactly resemble the one you'll create. Because of his profession and the natural connectivity among software techies, he opened up his primary, secondary, and tertiary circles to everyone without qualification. You may choose to be more selective. Still, this example illustrates the power of collaborative intellectual effort. There was tremendous enthusiasm, excitement, shared intent, and mutual benefit.

Rule Eight: Be Open to Different Collaborative Partners

Everyone gets stuck in ruts. People tend to partner with someone, the collaboration goes well, and they want to partner with them again. This is fine in one sense, but it can create problems if you limit yourself (consciously or not) to a few select collaborators. One of the reasons we encourage divergent connections is because they provide an opportunity for diverse collaborations. By exchanging and recombining your resources with different Networlding partners, you are exposed to more opportunities.

Cross-pollination is the key. You can only maximize the potential of your network if you explore it to its fullest. This means going forward with collaborations with different individuals who have different skills and interests. It might be difficult to do this in non-Networlding situations, but because you've "qualified" the individuals you know in terms of their intent and related goals and values, you can reasonably expect these collaborations to go well. No matter how different they are from you—whether they're in a different field, occupy higher or lower positions, are different ages, are known to you through personal or community connections—these individuals are operating on a similar relationship wavelength. You want to give yourself and your Networlding partners the most shots at the best opportunities, and this will only happen if you're open to different types of collaborations.

Let's say you're a business executive, and you decide to collaborate with a member of your primary circle who is a theater manager. Your firm will donate a percentage of sales of its product to this theater. Your firm obtains favorable publicity and sales, and the theater receives the funds needed to launch its new season. In turn, you get promoted to marketing manager based on the success of this collaboration, and then you're in a position to work with the theater manager on other, even more significant projects.

By being adventurous in your collaborations within Networlding parameters, you are likely to learn new skills and experience successes that would be denied you if you limited your collaborations to a familiar few.

Rule Nine: Strive for Networld Equality

Effective networlds produce continuous, beneficial exchanges and opportunities for all members. One-sided networks, in contrast, often collapse under the weight of people's resentments over not receiving their fair share.

Have you ever been involved in a one-sided relationship where you seemed to be doing all the giving or all the taking? After a while, you probably lost interest and drifted away. You became less willing to share your time and resources with the other person because you felt taken advantage of (too much giving) or guilty (too much taking). Sooner or later, the relationship fell apart.

The same thing happens in an unbalanced networld. If you have a primary circle of nine people and two of them are doing all the giving or taking, the circle cannot sustain itself. There needs to be fair and equal exchanges throughout the networld. Of course, it's impossible for fair and equal exchanges to occur all the time. At certain times, some members will be giving more than others. But over the course of a year or two, the exchanges should even out. If that doesn't happen then there's something wrong with your networld. It may be that one person is a pure taker and doesn't belong, or it may be that you need to move someone out of your primary circle who is too busy to give at the moment. You may even want to look for an entirely new networld to join if yours is untenable.

Of course, there's only so much you can do to achieve equality among your Networlding partners. As much as you try to involve everyone, you're at the mercy of other people's attitudes and behaviors. Still, it is important to follow this rule and expect others to follow it too. At the very least, you can call attention to someone who is doing a disproportionate amount of giving or taking and suggest that that individual's approach is disturbing the networld's equilibrium.

Rule Ten: Be Willing to Redefine Success

Networlding can lead to untraditional as well as traditional forms of success. Although it might help a person further a career in an organization, it can also provide a variety of other rewards and achievements. We know networlders who have used this process to discover new careers, who have found greater meaning and fulfillment from work, and who have learned to achieve in areas outside of traditional professional arenas (charitable work, artistic endeavors, politics, and so on).

What tends to happen with effective networlds is that horizons are broadened and new possibilities are explored. Many networlders tell us that it is a transforming experience. Because they receive so much support, get involved in so many exciting new projects, and discover interests and skills they never had before, their old view of success becomes too narrow. Although some people develop greater ambition in specific areas, others expand their definition of what constitutes success. For some, success includes being able to work at home and spend more time with their children.

This idea fits well in the new work scenario, where success doesn't necessarily mean a straight climb up the corporate ladder. Careers today more closely resemble moves on a chessboard where people go forward, backward, and sideways in order to fulfill their intent. They go from project to project and opportunity to opportunity, gaining knowledge, skills, and financial rewards. This kind of progress may not be steady or continuously vertical, but it provides a deeper sense of meaning and satisfaction.

Jennifer had spent fourteen years working for two large organizations in their human resource departments. Her driving ambition was to be a human resource director for a Fortune 100 company. When she started Networlding about a year ago, however, she began to redefine success. Her exposure to people outside of the human resource arena and her deep and meaningful exchanges with a wide variety of people (a rabbi, a doctor, and a wilderness guide were in her networld) caused her to reassess her career plans. She realized that working in human resources for a large company was no longer satisfying to her; she found the politics and the lack of freedom stifling. Through a Networlding connection, Jennifer had the opportunity to do some volunteer coaching for a women's group. She discovered that she not only loved doing it but also was good at it; she received very positive feedback. All this led Jennifer to redefine success as establishing an independent coaching practice for women-owned businesses, which she went on to do.

Let These Rules Be Your Guide

As you venture out into the real world, you need to look at people you know and for people you don't in order to create your networld and the resulting opportunities. The temptation to network instead of networld may be strong. It's easy to become discouraged about your job or career, and you may want to rush into finding someone to help. A full card file may seem better than nothing.

If you start feeling this way, these rules will help you. They will remind you of why Networlding will work for you in more meaningful ways than any superficial meet-and-greet approach. Look back over these rules as often as necessary as you start mapping out your Networlding strategy, which begins with creating a value-driven plan.

CHAPTER THREE

Step One: Establish a Values-Rich Foundation

Albert Einstein once said, "Try not to become a man of success, but rather a man of value." Values are the principles that guide your actions on a daily basis. This first step in the Networlding process is about becoming strongly aware of your values and creating goals that reflect these values. From a purely networking perspective, of course, this first step doesn't make much sense. What do values have to do with making contacts that lead to success in careers and at work?

The Networlding answer has to do with creating a foundation for lifelong success. You can't do this if you simply make connections with others who can do you some good now but are acting out of a sense of pure self-interest rather than principles. And you can't do it if you "use" someone to get what you want now with no consideration for helping that person get what he or she wants.

Networlding is a long journey rather than a short ride, and you want to make sure that those you share it with are people you truly feel connected to on a deeper level than money. The journey must be marked not only by your continuous success but by the success of others. This ongoing, mutual success won't be possible if your partners lack strong, solid values. Because Networlding relationships last for a long time, you won't have the impetus to help people who operate very differently than you do.

Once you establish a values-rich foundation, you'll have a base from which you can create goals. However, please don't misunderstand what we're asking you to do in this first step: we're *not* asking you to create your values. You've been developing your values all your life, displaying them through your actions. Even if you're just beginning your career, you've had ample opportunity to express these values in school, in summer jobs, and in your choice of profession. What you may not have done is identify these values consciously and translate them into actions.

This can be a scary first step. It requires personal reflection. Once your values emerge, you may choose to change jobs or even pursue a different career. But although this may be uncomfortable at first, it is part of a longer journey that will take you toward a much more satisfying, meaningful path, both personally and professionally.

Creating a Values Foundation

To get on the path toward establishing your values foundation, take these six actions:

- Decide what matters to you most.
- Identify your value priorities.
- Align your values with your actions.
- Create a personal charter.
- Set goals.
- Establish a one-year plan.

Decide What Matters to You Most

The things that are most important to you are your values. Sometimes, however, what's important to you on the surface is not really what's important deep down. Or perhaps you think that three or four things are equally important and fail to prioritize what's absolutely essential. Or prioritizing your values may be an issue you've never given much serious thought to. In all these cases, the result is confusion about your values, and this confusion will prevent you from finding the Networlding partners with whom you can form dynamic, long-lasting relationships. If you're not clear about your own values, how will you find someone whose values resonate with yours?

To determine what's important to you, take the following actions.

Write About What's Important in Your Life

Write out statements about the major things in your life that you deem important, for instance: "I love my job." "My spouse and my kids are what really matter to me." "Security is what I'm after." "I want to have fun." "I spend most of my free time working on my boat."

Rank-Order Your Priorities

Rank these statements in order of your priorities now: what's most important, what comes in second, and so on.

Double-Check Your Ratings

Check your rankings by asking yourself a question: If you had to choose between spending more time at Item 1 and less time at Item 2, would you spend more time at work and less time with family, for example? If you're unwilling to take time away from one thing on your list, then that's the one that should be ranked first.

Double-Check Them with a Friend

Finally, double-check your rankings with an empathic friend to see if your perceptions match how your friend perceives your value ranking. Often, friends can help clarify what matters most as they observe both your actions and your words.

Identify Your Value Priorities

What's most important to you translates into a set of prioritized values. For instance, if taking care of your family is most important, then two of your priorities might be *connection* and *security*. Identifying these values isn't an academic exercise; it directly affects who you choose for your networld and who selects you for theirs. Values are magnetic. Consider the *Trends Report* (1997) that revealed that 76 percent of consumers would buy from socially responsible companies rather than others if price and quality were equal. Just as people are drawn to organizations that have compatible values, they're drawn to individuals in the same way. If you identify your values and allow them to guide your actions, you will attract other people who have strong values. They may not be the same values as yours, but they will be compatible. For instance, you may value freedom above all else whereas another individual may value personal development. Each of you will respect and admire the other for following through on strongly held values, and a connection may be made.

Of course, if you don't define your values you're likely to establish relationships with people who operate from a valueless base. We've heard countless stories of people who entered into a partnership with an individual who ended up embezzling from the company, establishing unethical customer practices, or doing something that harmed the business. With hindsight, the honest people say, "I suspected something was wrong with that guy from the beginning." But the suspicion never was acted on because their own values weren't defined. If they were, these people would have realized that the prospective partners operated out of a very different framework and would never have gone into business with them.

Therefore, we'd like you to focus on what you listed as mattering most to you and then check two or three corresponding values from the following list (feel free to add other values if you wish):

Achievement

Advancement

Adventure

Competition

Connection

Cooperation

Creativity

Economic prosperity or security

Fame

Freedom

Friendship

Fun

Health

Integrity

Loyalty

Order (structure)

Personal development

Power
Recognition
Responsibility
Self-respect
Wisdom

Align Your Values with Your Actions

Once you've identified your values, you need to make sure your behaviors are consistent with them. If you haven't consciously thought about your value priorities until now, the odds are that your actions are inconsistent. For instance, let's say you value prosperity. To determine if your actions are consistent with this value, you need to ask yourself some questions: Have I gone back to school for an advanced degree that will help me earn more in the future? Have I talked to a financial planner about how I might save more annually (and if so, have I acted on her advice)? Have I been willing to look for another job or career with greater earnings potential?

Try the following exercise to create consistency between your values and actions:

- List your top three values.
- Write one strategy or action designed to reinforce each value.

Let's say that you value integrity. In this case, your strategy might be to "tell people at work what I really believe rather than what they want to hear." Although it's fine to list more than one strategy per value, make sure the strategies are doable. In other words, be confident that you can do them and are committed to implementing them soon.

We want to emphasize the importance of this exercise and the previous ones. We've found that people routinely fool themselves if they fail to formalize the process of defining and aligning their values. Remember Jennifer, the coach for women-owned businesses whom we met in the previous chapter? She operated out of her own home because she liked the freedom it gave her. In fact, she believed that freedom was what she valued most. But in fact Jennifer was not particularly happy with the freedom she'd achieved.

Many times, she found herself feeling isolated and regretting that she wasn't meeting a diverse group of people. She rationalized these problems as the price she had to pay for having her freedom. But after going through the values identification process described here, she realized that although freedom was an important value, a far more important one was connection. As one of her strategies, Jennifer resolved to look for "an assignment or opportunity where I can interact with different types of people." Within the month, she began working two days a week for a Silicon Valley Web development company that required her to meet regularly with both the development company executives and their customers. Jennifer maintained her freedom, but now her actions were much more consistent with the value of connection.

Create a Personal Charter

Once your values are aligned with your actions, you're in a good position to think in larger terms. Once you know what's important to you, consider the significance of your values and how they might be translated into your life's work. A charter is your mandate to act, an overarching statement that describes who you want to be, what you want to do, the profession or principle to which you want to dedicate your life, and the legacy you want to leave. This charter is designed to give you direction and guide you to networld partnerships that will help you accomplish your mission. It gives you the chance to take a leadership role in your life.

Create your charter by asking yourself the following three questions, keeping in mind the values you've already selected:

- What group of people do I want to help the most (managers, senior citizens, minorities, the mentally ill, children, and so on)?
- What one activity could I do for a lifetime, and do it tirelessly?
- Why would I want to engage in this activity?

Let's say you answered these questions this way:

- I want to help senior citizens.
- I love helping other people enjoy and learn from the fine arts (drawing, painting, and so on).

- I want to pursue this activity because I derive great satisfaction from helping others discover their ability to express themselves artistically.

In this case, your charter would be: *To help senior citizens draw and paint so they can gain satisfaction and joy from artistic expression.* This charter gives shape and substance to your values. It suggests a direction to pursue that will help you live your values. The next step is to become more specific about that direction.

Set Goals

You may have set goals in the past as part of your job or more generally as part of career or personal aspirations. What we're asking you to do here is set goals that flow from your values. Using your values expressed in your charter, map out appropriate goals.

It may make you uncomfortable to set these goals or you may find it hard to come up with them, but we urge you nevertheless to make an effort to do so. Unless you have specific goals, you'll find it difficult (if not impossible) to know which people can help you achieve them. To facilitate the goal-setting process, take an hour or two each week to write about what you would like to achieve. Keeping a journal is instructive because you can look back at what you've written at the end of each week. There will be a pattern that starts to form, a clear indication of what you really would like to achieve (and what doesn't mean much to you). One networlder named Pat used this strategy for a month; from it she came to realize her desire to move from a position as a sales executive to start her own consulting business. Today, she is very successful, seven years after determining how her top value of freedom meant owning her own company.

After determining this pattern, write down your goals. The only two stipulations we make are that (1) you be consistent with your values and as specific as possible, and (2) they be realistically achievable in one year or less. Beyond that, feel free to list any goals at all. Here are some examples: get a new job, be promoted, start my own business, take my company to the next level, find a new career, travel less, increase my sales, balance my life, find new friends, explore my spirituality.

Establish a One-Year Plan

Next, establish a one-year timetable for achieving each goal (the goals should range from one to three in number), and then work backward in three-month increments. We find that setting more than three goals when you first start Networlding can result in less success. For instance, let's take a person whose one-year goal is to get a sales job in a field where he believes in the products that he's selling. A nine-month goal for this person might be this: creating a list of twenty organizations whose culture, products, and services seem admirable. A six-month goal might be this: sending out letters and making calls to all the organizations on the list. A three-month goal might be this: scheduling interviews with at least three of these organizations. A zero-month goal might be this: getting a job offer from one of the organizations.

Facilitating the Construction of Your Values in a Values-Rich Foundation

Achieving any significant goal is challenging. Achieving one that has the additional overlay of values means that you've added a degree of difficulty (though a degree that's more than worth it). We recommend that aspiring networlders use certain tools and techniques to facilitate this first step. Here are four tactics that we think will prove helpful.

Identify and Rely on Your Strengths

Lead with your strength is a phrase that's particularly appropriate here. Networlders don't try to be what they're not—that's why they have partners. They focus on what they do best, and this helps them achieve the things they set out to do. No less a person than Winston Churchill relied on his strength of seemingly infinite patience during the months when the war seemed lost; he did not lose his head and take rash actions but rather waited for his strategy to work.

What's astonishing is that many people aren't certain what their strengths are. If you're in doubt, ask friends, family, and colleagues about your talents and skills. You'll find a surprising unanimity of opinion. Once you're aware of what your strength is, use it. For instance, if everyone agrees that your strength is your artistic ability, design terrific cover letters to achieve your three-month goal of getting five interviews with art directors at ad agencies.

Broadcast your strengths to make prospective networlders aware of how you could contribute to an alliance. We call this process "bridging." It is the process of communicating to those in your networld your unique strengths. As you go after your goals, you want the people who can help you to know what it is you do that might also help them. In other words, you share the value you bring to the relationship.

Make Sure Your Goals Are Catalysts

Networlders may make mistakes as they move toward their goals, but they're mistakes of action rather than passivity. You need to compel yourself to act, and one easy way to do this is by making sure your goals motivate you to do something rather than just sit there. Doug Mellinger set a goal of starting his own Internet software company within one year, but his catalytic goal was an interim one that involved contacting the thirty most powerful chief information officers about his concept. Just the idea of talking to these incredible people excited Doug, and he wrote each of them asking that person to be his mentor. Two responded and agreed to help him. Within four years his growing company had $10 million in sales.

Ask yourself: Does my goal make me want to do something? Does it cause me to want to act immediately, even if it's logistically impossible to do so? If not, it may be that your goal doesn't fit with a high-priority value. Or perhaps you haven't been specific enough in writing down the goal.

Test the Reality of Your Plan

Yes, networlders think big, but they also are realists. One of the dangers of creating values-based goals is that they can be overly idealistic. If your value is independence and you set the goal to start your own company, you may become so caught up in the value ("What's important to me more than anything else is to grow my own company, and I'll do anything to make this happen") that you lose sight of some basic realities. What realistically may take two years, you try to do in one. Or you underestimate the capital expenditures necessary to get it launched.

Temper the idealism that comes from following your values by putting them to the "rest test." After you write a plan, put it in a drawer and don't look at it or think about it for three days. At the end of that time, take it out and look at it with fresh eyes. You'll find that you can view it with much greater objectivity after you've removed yourself from it for a few days and given your mind a rest.

Another good Networlding technique is to gather a team of advisers to review your plan on an informal basis. Ask them to review it from all angles. Do they think you have the time and resources to accomplish what you've outlined? Do they believe your goals are consistent with your values and charter?

Margo Pachona, the head of the speakers' bureau Connections Unlimited in Chicago, did just that when she started her business. One of her goals was to be in the black after six months, and she knew this was perhaps overly ambitious. To test her assumptions, she brought together a diverse group of meeting planners, consultants, and speakers. They supported her assessment, and because of the experience some were encouraged to become part of Margo's networld. Today, five years later, Margo is still booking a number of those speakers who helped her in those early days. Margo says, "There are also clients, meeting planners who hire my speakers, who gave me wonderful advice when I first began. And they still continue to provide support and encouragement."

Adjust to the Discomfort

As creatures of habit, we have difficulty with significant change in our lives. Many of us may find it uncomfortable to change our behaviors so that they are aligned with our values and to pursue value-based goals that are different from those we are used to pursuing. We want to assure you that this discomfort will lessen over time. If you stick with your plan, you'll develop new habits and approaches that will create a new comfort level.

Harvey, for example, decided he would pursue his value of economic prosperity and security by leaving his current job and taking another that required him to be much more aggressive and ambitious than he had ever been before. He created a series of goals for his first year on the job; one of them was to contact the one hundred top prospects in his region. At first, Harvey was intimidated by this task and found it awkward trying to make contact with not only a new group of prospects but prospects in bigger companies and with more influence than he was used to. Though his discomfort level was high, he gritted his teeth and stuck with it, reminding himself of his charter: to create a better, more secure life for himself and his family. Finally, after about two months, people started returning his calls and Harvey found that he was making inroads at a few companies. By being persistent and sticking to his plan, his contacts snowballed, and soon it felt like second nature to deal with bigger organizations and top executives.

Besides being persistent, use your journal to help you become comfortable with your new values-based plan. This activity helps you put your discomfort in perspective and also eases the pain that comes with any change. Expressing your feelings about your charter, goals, values, and new behaviors is a stress-reducing activity. It gives you the chance to poke and prod (in writing) the values that you've decided matter most and the goals that flow from those values. It allows you to express all your doubts and uncertainties as well as your hopes and dreams. Putting them down on paper and reflecting on what you've written lets you take stock of your values. What usually happens is that the discomfort you feel about living those values lessens a bit when you articulate them; the new, unfamiliar things you're doing seem less foreign when you formally analyze them.

Subscribing to Networlding Beliefs

A values-based plan will naturally lead you to other people who are pursuing dreams rooted in their strong values. People notice and respect those who are going through life with a clear purpose. They become aware of the confidence with which you go after your goals and the courage you show in following your values wherever they take you. You'll find that certain types of people especially will gravitate toward you and ultimately become part of your networld. They're the ones who have also built a values-rich foundation (or aspire to do so).

Sometimes, however, it's difficult to identify prospective networlders based on values. After all, their values (and goals) may be significantly different from your own; it may seem as if you have little in common. We've found that although networlders' values are often different, their beliefs are usually similar. They create a "community of faith," people who adhere to the same tenets of success, purpose, and process. Shared beliefs are important because they unite people who may be very different in other ways. Beliefs provide the cement of Networlding relationships. Although your values are often shaped at an early age, your beliefs evolve over time. Besides providing a link to other networlders, your beliefs will inspire and motivate you, helping you move toward your goals. We'd like you to become familiar with the following networld beliefs and determine which ones you subscribe to. If they are ones that seem difficult to accept or you're not sure about them, we ask you to reflect on them and try to incorporate them into your belief system. The beliefs are these:

- Anything is possible with the support of others.
- It's important to make a difference.
- You get what you ask for.
- All resources will be provided to reach your goals.
- Life is filled with abundance and opportunities.
- There must be mutual rewards for partners.

Anything Is Possible with the Support of Others

Networlders aren't loners or rugged individualists but rather people who truly believe in the power of teamwork, partnerships, alliances, and other types of groups. They don't pursue goals alone and single-handedly but with an eye toward linking with other people in order to achieve them. Ultimately, what they believe in is the potential of relationships to achieve great things—things that might be out of reach if they were to go it alone.

Here are two examples. Carol Hansen and Victor Grey began the Only Love Prevails World Peace Experiment in 1998, a grassroots effort to achieve global peace. It may sound like an absurdly ambitious goal, but Carol and Victor have already enlisted the support of forty-two hundred people in forty-eight countries, and using the Internet and other sources believe they'll have eighty thousand people signed up by the year 2000.

The second example is a much smaller-scale but no less significant effort. Golda Meir, the former prime minister of Israel, grew up in Milwaukee. At age twelve, she attended a school where there were a number of students from low-income households. Knowing that many of these students couldn't afford to buy the books the school required, she used money she had saved from her allowance to rent a hall and then held a fundraiser there that helped these students purchase their books.

It Is Important to Make a Difference

Making a difference means affecting other people's lives in a significant, meaningful way. This belief motivates people to set goals that benefit others and be on the lookout for opportunities to make a difference in the lives of family, friends, coworkers, and the community.

It's not surprising, therefore, that many networlders are volunteers for not-for-profit or political organizations and other groups. They're eager to find an outlet for their skills and knowledge that can make a difference for the disadvantaged, the mentally handicapped, and society at large. A side benefit of volunteering is that it gives them the opportunity to demonstrate their skills and knowledge to a new group of people. We know more than one networlder who has developed a crucial career relationship by working with someone as a volunteer.

A commitment to making a difference can manifest itself in work situations. C. William Pollard, president of Service Master, a company with annual revenues of over $5 billion, has inculcated the idea of making a difference into the corporate culture. Up and down the line, people who make an impact and help others are rewarded. In fact, this philosophy is carved in stone in the company's lobby: "Your input, no matter how small or large, makes a difference."

You Get What You Ask For

Networlders aren't shy about speaking up and communicating their needs and goals. This doesn't mean they believe in arrogantly asking for the moon when it's clearly out of their reach. Acting on their values, however, provides them with great confidence. It gives them the feeling that they're doing the right thing. As a result, they feel compelled to ask for a lot and expect to get it. This is confidence not only in themselves but in their goals and values.

When Ray Silverstein sold his manufacturing company, he started a training and consulting firm called Presidents Resource Organization (PRO) that provides support and instruction for presidents of small businesses. When he began calling on these individuals, Ray asked that they commit both time and money to deal with management and leadership issues that many of them had never dealt with before. It was asking a lot, but Ray now has established eight PRO groups in the Chicago area with plans to franchise the organization nationally.

It's important to note that networlders like Ray view this asking process as a reciprocal one. They are confident that they can ask for a significant amount because they're willing to give a significant amount in return. Ray exchanged his years of experience for a commitment by business owners to reciprocate their time and dollars.

All Resources Will Be Provided to Reach Your Goals

Networlders operate with a mind-set of plenty rather than scarcity. They don't fret about how little money there is or how they lack the technology or information necessary to achieve a goal. Instead, they move forward with a sense that they can tap into the resources they need. This facilitates the Networlding process because it makes these individuals willing to ask for resources from all the people in their networld. Once again, however, this is a reciprocal process; they're perfectly willing to share their resources with others.

Certainly this doesn't mean that networlders foolishly embark on a venture without the slightest idea of where funding will come from. Rather, networlders don't let the lack of funding defeat them; they move forward cautiously but with a belief that their venture is sound and that they will attract funding if they continue to ask for it.

Life Is Filled with Abundance and Opportunities

One of the things we've observed about traditional networkers is that they believe there are certain places and situations reserved for making connections and doing business. To them, life isn't filled with abundance and opportunity as much as very narrowly defined situations are. In contrast, networlders are open to all sorts of opportunities and possibilities, recognizing not only that relationships are formed in unusual places but also that there are more productive relationships to be formed than anyone has time for.

Here is an illustration: In the lobby of a four-star hotel, a man from Finland and one from Russia are engrossed in a conversation about tourism. In the nearby dining room, a newspaper reporter from the Yukon is discussing fish farming with a Norwegian administrator. These people and others from around the world have gathered for the Northern Forum's board of directors meeting. Northern Forum members talk about issues of mutual interest to inhabitants of the Northern Hemisphere, from circumpolar air routes to shorebird migration. As a result of the most recent forum, Alaskan and Sakhalin scientists are working together to identify environmental risks in Sakhalin that could threaten both countries, and Norway has sold aluminum boats to Sakhalin that work well in icy conditions.

None of these people would have taken the trouble to meet unless they believed that life is filled with abundance and opportunities. A sense of possibility drew the members of the forum together—the possibility of finding an opportunity with someone else who brought a very different perspective and very different ideas to the table.

There Must Be Mutual Rewards for Partners

This belief goes beyond quid pro quo. Networlders continuously think about how they can help others in their networld. They focus on mutual rather than individual rewards. They possess a high degree of sensitivity about what their partners' time constraints are, what they're interested in, and who to link them up with. They are highly respectful of each and every partner.

This belief is based on the fact that networlds grow together rather than apart. In other words, the overall gain is greater if everyone benefits rather than if only one person does. When everyone wins, the partnership and the networld are strengthened. When only one person wins, the alliance weakens because of resentment and envy.

In the real world, creating mutual rewards means freely sharing ideas, information, and other resources. This is what will help others in your networld achieve their goals. Mary, a vice president at a large pharmaceutical company, routinely shares her information with five other vice presidents as well as four or five other people in her networld outside the company. At Mary's company, this is an unusual practice—most of the vice presidents hoard their information.

Certainly Mary helped the people in her networld take advantage of opportunities and develop strategies by giving them important pieces of data. But Mary too benefited from her belief in mutual rewards. People came to view her as a wise person. Her generosity with knowledge earned her a reputation as being "smart and informed." At meetings, supervisors regularly asked her for her ideas and named her to head teams. One of the recipients of Mary's information was a supplier, and her insights helped that supplier save her company millions of dollars. It wasn't long before Mary received a well-deserved promotion (not to mention more than one job offer).

The Story of a Budding Networlder

Lowell Wightman's transition from business consultant to basketball coach illustrates many of the principles discussed here. Many of you will not make such a radical career transition to establish a values-rich foundation. But as you will see Lowell was clearly driven to live his values, and as a result he set goals for himself, formed beliefs, and found that he was connecting with an entirely new group of people who became part of his networld.

After twenty years as a consultant, Lowell began to realize that his values and life were out of synch. This realization wasn't an epiphany but one that evolved as he volunteered as a coach for his son's baseball team. As his son approached high school graduation, Lowell realized that he would miss helping the young people on the team. What he valued, he came to realize, revolved around helping others. Although he could do that to a certain extent as a consultant, consulting didn't offer the type of personal and skill development that he prioritized. Or as Lowell put it, "Showing people techniques that improve their performance has consumed my professional life, but when a young person smiles at me or screams with joy at their accomplishments, that is a pure emotion with no strings attached, and I feel great." Thus, he set the goal of becoming a college basketball coach. He created interim goals, such as gaining experience coaching sports on a high school level, which he has already achieved. His Networlding belief that "it's important to make a difference" has helped him pursue his goals and given him the courage to approach people in a very different sphere of life than he was used to.

Lowell is still building his networld as he moves toward his ultimate goal, and he's doing it consciously, confidently, and with his values in mind. By doing so, Lowell—like you—must now look beyond contacts for true connections.

CHAPTER FOUR

Step Two: Make Connections for Your Primary Circle

Values will help you establish the deeper connections with people that Networlding requires. Rather than forming superficial relationships at the drop of a hat, you'll form meaningful relationships more slowly and thoughtfully. The values you're now conscious of will guide you toward other people with compatible values.

This doesn't mean, however, that you can sit back and wait for relationships to develop through "value magic." You need to be proactive and develop a strategy to establish relationships with compatible people. During Step Two, you create a list of potential networld connections and winnow it down to its essence based on emotional, business, and cognitive factors as well as values. Doing this will yield deep, strong relationships that will not only contribute to your professional success but also add richness to the quality of your life.

The Difference Between Contacts and Connections

Networkers have contacts; networlders have connections. As we've already explained, the difference has to do with the depth of the relationships and how they're achieved. Networkers traditionally rely on the *funnel effect:* they attempt to funnel as many people as possible into their lives, hoping that a high quantity of interactions will produce a few good opportunities in the end. In contrast, networlders spend more time up front building a relatively small number of relationships that will eventually produce better and longer-lasting opportunities. Just like the companies that know that 20 percent of their customers produce 80 percent of their business, networlders recognize that a targeted approach works best. If they can form connections with the right people, they will reap incredible benefits.

Discernment is key in understanding what we mean by connections. If you are discerning, you look at prospective relationships perceptively. To form a meaningful connection, you must assess a potential relationship based on what will be exchanged. Will you and your partner provide each other with support? Will the relationship be strictly business, or can you count on the other person to be on the same emotional wavelength and share feelings about a problem or opportunity? We've seen networkers who are pure ladder-climbers and have no meaningful relationships. Even if they succeed (and success is a challenge to sustain because their relationships often are flimsy and short term), it's often an empty success. These people aren't discerning in their relationships; they just form them without a second thought.

You need to decide which people among your contacts you can establish a meaningful connection with. Part of the discernment process is opening your mind to different relationship possibilities. Networkers tend to think narrowly: "I'm in the software business, so the people I need to form relationships with are software executives." Networlders embrace a world of relationship possibilities—from next-door neighbors to cubicle partners to clients to family members. Once you are aware of all these possibilities, you increase your odds of finding the people with whom you will establish tremendous relationships.

Your goal in Step Two is to create a primary circle (which will ultimately include up to ten people) all of whom belong to divergent groups—groups that represent different industries or interests—and one that includes influencers, that is, leaders in their respective fields. Networkers tend to focus on redundant groups, making contacts with people who have overlapping interests. Divergent groups open up numerous opportunities that networkers never are exposed to. The process of forming your primary networld circle starts with a simple task that most people overlook.

Identify Your Current Contacts

Though you may not realize it, you currently possess a powerful and wide-ranging set of contacts. It may include your mother who knows a high school principal who is interested in using you as a consultant. It may include the parent of your child's friend who owns a company at which you'd be interested in working. It may include a supplier at work who can introduce you to a great sales prospect. In other words, you need to identify your contacts holistically.

A good term to describe this expanded focus is *horizon of observability*. This is the foreseeable number of people connected to those whom you meet. You need to develop your ability to see not only those whom you meet but those whom they know, and so on. For instance, if you have a strong relationship with Anne, you may not think about the relationship you might establish with her friend Joe, or the relationship you might establish with Joe's friend Sue. Through our relationships with just a few people, we're potentially connected to thousands of others. Networlders develop the ability to see these connections.

First, you need to identify your highest-potential Networlding relationships. Doing this will give you a sense of who can help you achieve your goals and whom you can help. Essentially, you want to build this baseline group first so that you can eventually pick and choose from it to form your primary group.

The following exercise will help you create your baseline group. List all the people you interact with in the following categories: family, friends, colleagues, customers and clients, vendors, professional service providers (accountant, lawyer, real estate agent, and so on). Extend your list by adding the names of people you have met at conferences, while traveling, on vacation, in community or volunteer activities. You now should have a sizable list of names that requires some discernment to translate them all into solid relationships.

Identify Qualities You Want in a Networlding Partner

To focus your list, you need to determine which people possess the qualities you are looking for in a Networlding partner. This requires a bit of thinking. Start out by reviewing the values you outlined in Step One and their associated goals. Then look back and think back about the people you created a successful venture with (not just in the business sense, but in school, in volunteer activities, and so on) who had values that were compatible with yours. For instance, your study partner in school went beyond the call of duty, making an effort to ensure you understood assignments and telephoning when she thought you might be having trouble with a particular issue. You both got good grades in the class, and you felt you had a bond of caring and accountability and were both eager to share knowledge. This individual fits the bill.

Now create a list of ten people with whom you have achieved this kind of success together or who have supported you in accomplishing something. Next to the person's name, write down the qualities about him or her that you valued the most. For example:

Top Ten People Qualities

1. Susan   Great listener, appreciative
2. Andrew   Excellent strategist
3. John   Strong financial skills
4. Mary   Great ability to see opportunities
5. Cari   Great sense of humor, connection-conscious
6. Laura   Strong analytical skills
7. Julie   Always thinks of others, empathetic
8. Bart   Great at building rapport
9. Jeremy   Excellent communication skills
10. Taylor   Wonderful salesperson, very responsible

Now it's your turn:

Top Ten People Qualities

1.
2.
3.
4.
5.
6.
7.
8.
9.
10.

Next, answer the following questions, but answer only after you've reflected on your list:

- What one quality of all those listed do you most admire?
- What two additional qualities are important to you?
- Which of these qualities have you shared with others and found that others greatly appreciated?

Given the qualities that are important to you and the ones you possess, you can now think about those among your baseline group who would be good people to establish deeper relationships with. Before making your choices, remember that you want to focus on the three qualities you most admire and the ones that are complementary to your qualities. In terms of the former, it's simply a matter of identifying those people who possess the qualities you consider to be key. In terms of the latter, you want to determine who has a quality that dovetails with your own. For instance, when David Packard partnered with Bill Hewlett to start what became the megacompany Hewlett-Packard, the relationship worked because their very different qualities meshed perfectly: Packard was a great "outside" relationship-builder whereas Hewlett was brilliant at building strong employee relationships.

Think of other partnerships you have seen—for instance, Katharine Hepburn, whose incredible talent complemented her favorite partner, Spencer Tracy. Hepburn was wonderful on screen, as she caught Tracy's frequent snappy remarks like an adept catcher in a ballgame and scored home runs with some equally powerful retorts. Their relationship worked well because they were well suited for one another.

With this in mind, put a checkmark next to the people whose qualities you both admire and believe will mesh with your own.

Screen People for Networlding Traits

As you determine those with whom you should form a connection, it's helpful to search for certain identifying traits. Not everyone in positions of power and influence will be good Networlding partners. Similarly, individuals who are outside of the traditional networking circle may make excellent networlders.

We describe the following traits to help you recognize a good networlder when you meet one as well as to help you become familiar with the traits you need to develop in yourself.

Supportive

Some people are only supportive of their own achievements or only demonstrate enthusiasm for your success if they will reap some of the benefits. In contrast, networlders enjoy making you look good. When you tell them about your success, they want to celebrate. When you talk to them about a problem you're having, they're eager to lend an ear or a hand. In short, they listen, encourage, and lend whatever assistance is required and enjoy sharing in your triumphs.

Continuous Communicators

Networkers tend to call when they need you. Networlders call regularly, whether or not there's a mutual opportunity. As Mark Twain observed, "The best time to make a friend is before you need one." Or to put it in Networlding terms, you need to have the relationship established before the opportunity arrives. Relationships flourish when there's continuous communication. Making the effort to keep a partner informed and aware helps relationships grow and builds trust. This is an indispensable trait of networlders and one that you can easily identify: just ask yourself how often someone calls you, and why.

Reliable and Responsible

These people do what they say they're going to do when they say they're going to do it. They're responsive to requests and effective in carrying out tasks. Another way of putting this is that they take their responsibilities seriously. This is as opposed to someone who offers all sorts of excuses about time constraints and other commitments in order to justify not doing something he promised to do. Ultimately, this means taking responsibility for a relationship and taking it seriously.

Influential

We define influence as the power to affect another person, a group of people, or the course of events. Although influence may be based on wealth, position, or prestige, its Networlding basis is usually ability. Networlders have some expertise that they're willing to employ on another person's behalf—to help someone make a deal, find information, analyze a situation, meet another person, and so on. People of influence are often experts and leaders in their respective fields or they have some area where they're highly respected for their abilities. Furthermore, influence isn't a passive quality. You might possess influence but rarely if ever be willing to use it. Networlders use their influence regularly on behalf of their partners. We will talk more about influencers in the next chapter.

Knowledgeable

We're not referring only to people who know a lot but rather to people who have *done* a lot. Networlders have had rich and varied experiences that, when combined with their "hard" knowledge, can be truly useful to their partners. The Internet makes "facts" accessible to everyone, but it cannot make experience accessible. People who can draw conclusions from and tell stories about their experiences can teach you a great deal. Knowledge exchanges between networlders are more than exchanges of data; they involve sharing stories that illuminate concepts far better than any dry recitation of facts can.

Active Listener

To listen actively to someone is a head-and-heart collaboration. Active listening is not just absorbing words with one's mind and responding analytically but opening one's heart and responding emotionally; it means being totally present during each conversation. This active listening quality is something all networlders need to work at. It means that you can't just listen and provide token comments but must really try to understand what a person is saying—the fears, hopes, concerns, and dreams beneath the words—and offer feedback that reflects this deeper understanding.

People who possess the active listening trait energize others with their attentiveness. Oliver Wendell Holmes put it best (if we remember correctly): "When we listen to people there is an alternating current, and this recharges us so that we never get tired of each other . . . and it is this little creative fountain inside us that begins to spring and cast up new thoughts and unexpected laughter and wisdom."

Empathic

This quality goes hand in hand with being a good listener. It's the ability to communicate that you feel what another is feeling, and it's a way of providing support. It is not the same as the false expressions of support that people in power sometimes receive. For example, we know one top executive who left a corporation and was immediately contacted by a number of people who told him they understood how difficult the transition must be and would do anything they could for him. But the executive perceived their expressions of support as contrived empathy; he felt they just wanted to take advantage of his corporate contacts for their own purposes. This was mainly because these people had not kept in contact with him regularly prior to his leaving.

For networlders, the person always comes before the opportunity. They're empathic because they care about the person, not because they care about taking advantage of him or her to get to the opportunity.

Appreciative

This may be a somewhat "smaller" trait than some of the others, but it's integral nevertheless to a Networlding relationship. Showing appreciation can be as simple as saying thank you for a referral or writing a note that eloquently expresses gratitude to someone who took you out to lunch. These gestures are important cumulatively rather than as single events; they gather weight, making people feel that their efforts are truly meaningful and valued by another.

Connection-Conscious

You've probably known people who have a knack for seeing and making connections. They recognize that two people should be introduced, and they act on that recognition. Sometimes it's as simple as an intuitive sense that they would work well together or that their interests and skills dovetail. Other times, the connection-conscious individual brings people together to achieve a specific goal. Networlders have their antennae up for possible connections, and they're not bashful about introducing a partner to someone else.

Rex Lewis, a noted tennis instructor, trainer, and speaker whose clients include Clint Eastwood, Merv Griffin, and Luciano Pavarotti, is extraordinarily connection-conscious. He's observed that people often don't see the connections they have with each other. Usually they can only see the most obvious things, like an interest in the same field or a desire to land the same client. Rex has trained himself to see the more subtle but often no less significant linkages and helps people realize that they might have more in common than they think. He is what we call a "maestro," an individual who creates a veritable orchestration of opportunities through linking people from divergent backgrounds and circles.

Finding the Individuals Who Will Help You Start Your Networld

Earlier we asked you to list ten people with whom you've had some success and the qualities you valued in them. We'd like you to take that list and think about it again, this time with the overlay of the Networlding traits we just discussed. It may be that some of the people you put on your earlier list lack these traits. Or it may be that your earlier list was too narrowly focused on people with whom you do business. What we're asking you to do here is edit as well as expand on that original list by examining different categories of potential Networlding partners:

Friends

Friends are often excluded from work-related networks on the theory that business and pleasure don't mix. We've known people who have said, "I don't want to bring my friend into this deal because if it doesn't work it will jeopardize the friendship." There are many problems with this point of view, not the least of which is that if people won't be your friends because a deal didn't work, they might not be worth having as friends in the first place. The other big issue is that networking relationships aren't conducive to friendships. Because they exist on a relatively superficial level, there's not much room for sharing feelings and thoughts that don't relate to the business at hand.

Networlders have a more holistic relationship with their partners. Although they may not be close friends, the lines between business and personal are often blurred. There is a camaraderie and a closeness that defines these relationships.

Therefore, do consider friends as candidates for your networld. We've found that there are tremendous unexplored opportunities waiting to be discovered in relationships with friends. For example, Joe, an accountant for a midsize accounting firm, was talking to his friend Harry, a contractor, about how much he enjoyed doing the accounting work on a volunteer basis for his son's hockey team. He told Harry a number of stories about hockey rinks and the costs associated with them. A few weeks later Harry landed a client who wanted him to construct an ice skating rink. The client needed someone to analyze the cost projections, and Harry immediately recommended Joe.

Family Members

Family members are sometimes more difficult to integrate into networlds than friends because of preexisting tensions and other difficulties (for instance, one brother may wonder why his sister included another brother in her network but not him). Still, we've found that family members can make terrific partners if the situation is right. You know your family members well and can immediately determine if they embody the traits of networlders and if their values are consistent with yours. If so, it may be worth putting them on your list.

Colleagues

These are the most logical Networlding partners, given their proximity and common area of work interest. On the plus side, you have a good sense of who these people are in work situations and are familiar with their skills, personalities, how they perform under pressure, and so on. But you might be unaware of their values or some of the other qualities we've discussed. Work situations often provide a limited view of an individual; they're operating under relatively narrow parameters there. There's a lot you don't know about the people you work with. For instance, we know an executive who never realized his direct report was an incredibly inventive and risk-taking individual because his job responsibilities never required these kinds of skills. It's also possible that a colleague has some unpleasant traits that were never revealed but might come out in a less limited collaboration.

In addition, many people work in your department or company who you probably don't know or don't know well. The odds are that some of them are highly compatible with you and could serve as a good partner. Because you already have an employer in common, it makes sense to initiate contact with people who you sense might be operating on the same "value wavelength" as you or who possess qualities that would make them good networlders.

Your colleagues also offer the opportunity to share confidential information on a regular basis. Dr. Colleen Braun, an international consultant and psychologist, understands the benefit of forming trusting bonds with colleagues. She shares her unique story of how she built relationships with trusted colleagues internationally:

My Middle East network opened doors for me elsewhere in the world through established professional networks. A brigadier in the military of the Arab Emirates would refer me to his friend, a brigadier in Southeast Asia. And so the networks grew. Interestingly, my network in the States began as an extension of my international relationships. One of the most fascinating and helpful U.S. contacts was initiated through a mutual friend in Saudi.

In 1989 I developed cancer. Not a "bad" cancer as those things go, but sufficient to scare and incapacitate me for half a year. While I was recovering back in the States, I noticed that the European and North American friends began to withdraw. We never talked about "it," and I felt as if I were isolated from their world by some sort of invisible but impenetrable bubble. Not so with my network in Asia and the Middle East. The phone calls were incessant. They asked about my fears, they offered encouragement, they talked of the "unspeakable." I didn't feel so alone because of their concern and honesty. But when I returned to my international assignment, all relationships changed because of this new experience, the vulnerabilities I had revealed.

Which colleagues have you built some trust with, shared general work-related information or perhaps more delicate information with, or helped through a crisis, as Dr. Braun's Asian and Middle-Eastern colleagues supported her?

Look at your colleagues carefully before adding them to your list. Talk to them about their interests and beliefs to get a better sense of how they stack up from a Networlding perspective. Colleagues are obviously a rich source for networlders, but you need to screen the prospects before writing down their names.

Customers

We know countless stories of people who have terrific relationships with customers that eventually extended beyond the traditional buy-and-sell transaction to become true Networlding collaborations. Mary, for instance, was a saleswoman at a medical products supply company who connected with Joan, a purchasing executive for a large hospital group. After a number of conversations, it was clear that Mary and Joan had much in common, from their interest in primitive art to their love of cooking. In fact, Joan had a small business on the side where she made and sold her pastries to local bakeries, and Mary contributed some recipes and volunteered to make some informal sales calls to bakeries in her neighborhood on Joan's behalf. Joan, who was about eight years older than Mary, took on a mentor role and not only provided Mary with leads for business at other hospitals but also made suggestions that helped Mary provide better service to her customers. Mary's rapid rise in her company—she became head of her sales team in less than three years—was due in part to her productive relationship with Joan; meanwhile, Joan soon had a flourishing baking business that eventually allowed her to quit her job and work at it full time.

Think about which of your customer relationships go beyond the norm. Are there people with whom you feel a kinship, people you really look forward to calling? Are there customers you'd really like to know better because you suspect their perspective on life and work is similar to your own? Have you found that they understand your business better than you do or that they have certain knowledge or skills that would contribute to your growth? If so, they may make good connections.

Vendors

Like customers, vendors may be more than one part of the buy-sell equation. The key here is getting past the view that vendors are always "trying to sell me something" and see other aspects of who they are. Howard, a CEO for a small manufacturing company, realized that he was burdened by this narrow view and invited all his vendors to what he privately termed "my first Networlding lunch." The lunch was a revelation. The vendors not only provided him with insights about his industry but talked about at least three people—a consultant, an advertising agency executive, and a trade industry magazine publisher—who Howard was excited about meeting. They were more than happy to make the connections for Howard, and after the meeting his relationships with two of the vendors deepened and became tremendously beneficial for everyone involved.

Casual Acquaintances

In the course of a week, most of us meet scores of people about whom we don't give a second thought. At trade shows, school events, parties, family gatherings, conferences, meetings, and a variety of other events, we have numerous brief encounters. Most of us fail to analyze these encounters and explore whether they might lead to productive partnerships. Although some of them may well lead nowhere, others have potential and should not be ignored. Just about every professional person who travels a great deal has a story about meeting someone on a plane and how that chance meeting turned into a great opportunity.

Obviously, we all have too many casual acquaintances to follow up on each and every one. What we're suggesting is that you not be quick to dismiss all of them. If a conversation goes well or you sense that an individual possesses Networlding qualities, exchange business cards at the very least. Or try arranging lunch or e-mailing each other. The idea is to test the casual acquaintance and see if it holds up under a little more contact. If it does, you may want to include this person on your list.

Using Instinct and Analysis to Create Your List of Connections

Even though we offer all these tips, we don't want to reduce creating your networld to a rigorously scientific process. To a certain extent, you need to rely on the guidelines we've offered and then use your own judgment. Review what you've designated as your values, goals, and plans; consider the qualities you determined you want in a networld partner and the qualities that networlders generally possess; and go over the categories you can use to make connections. Then start listing people who strike you as good candidates. Once you've created this list, you can use the following methods to help you further discover potential networld partners.

Determine Whether Someone Is an Exchanger or a Taker

Networlding is not about giving alone or taking alone. It's about exchanging. An *exchanger* is a person who understands the dynamic cycle of giving and receiving. Although not all networlders are selfless, they have an eagerness to continuously exchange leads, information, ideas, and so on. This understanding is critical to success. (See Figure 4.1.)

Review your list and see if each person is more a taker or more an exchanger.

- Exchangers ask questions that demonstrate a concern for your issues and needs. Takers ask questions that are focused on meeting their own issues and needs.
- Exchangers attempt to make sure that there is an equal exchange of information, leads, and so on. Takers always ask for business.
- Exchangers call you as much as you call them; they make an effort to stay in touch. Takers only call when they need something.

Figure 4.1. The Networlder Pyramid.

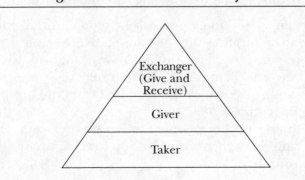

- Exchangers provide assistance without ever talking about how much they're doing for you or how much effort they're putting into it. Takers frequently complain that your project is taking too much time and say they hope you'll be able to reciprocate when they need you.

Assess the Relationship to See If There Is an Emotional Connection

As the Networlding support exchange model shows (see Chapter One), emotional connections are the base upon which successful relationships are built. Jeri is a successful advertising executive who has a small but powerful group of professional friendships, as she terms her networld. These are people with whom she shares both personal challenges as well as professional ones. If you ask Jeri what she attributes her success to, she points to her networld, sharing stories about how these friends have provided the emotional support necessary to survive the ups and downs of corporate life.

Think about whether there's any chemistry between you and the person on your list. Obviously, if you don't know the person well it's difficult to know if an emotional connection exists. But you can ask yourself a few questions: Do you feel that you and the other person are operating on the same wavelength? Or does it seem as if you're speaking two different languages? Another way of analyzing this issue is this: If you and this person had no business connection whatsoever, would you still want to be friends with him or her?

Determine If You Will Enjoy Working with the Individual

Networlders enjoy working together. The old networking notion is that it's fine to do business with people you hate as long as the deal gets done. In contrast, networlders like working with their partners. Bill Gates and Paul Allen, the founders of Microsoft, were very close, and their partnership benefited from the fun they had in building the company.

Think about whether people are fun to work with. Do their work habits and idiosyncrasies drive you nuts, or are they a pleasure to be around?

Refine to the Top Ten

Most people have overstuffed Rolodexes. It's impossible to manage so many relationships. We simply don't have the time or energy to develop hundreds of meaningful, committed partnerships. In fact, many of us tend to be so overwhelmed by all the names in our Rolodex that we don't know where or how to start building real relationships.

To begin growing your network, refine your list of connections to ten: this is your primary circle. If you find it difficult to cut your list to that number, use some practical considerations. Who on your list simply doesn't have the time or ability at the moment to form a relationship (they may be overwhelmed with work, taking care of a newborn, and so on)?

If you need another tiebreaker, try this technique: Write down the names of two people who are on the edge and then compare them in the categories of values, qualities that are important to you, networlder qualities, exchanger qualities, emotional connection with you, and fun to be with. Place a checkmark next to the person who has a more positive score than the other in each of the six categories. The person with fewer checkmarks should be eliminated from the list.

You should now have a list of ten potential partners. Don't let the list gather dust! Instead, next to each name write the current status of your relationship (for example, "colleague—talk to her sporadically") and list at least one action step for developing and exploring the relationship ("meet for lunch").

If you have fewer than ten people in your primary circle you still have a good basis to grow a strong networld. The secret is to form strong bonds with those chosen few who have the potential to exchange with you.

This step will get you started. Remember, though, that this is just a start. The next part of the process involves deepening these connections and evolving new connections from them. This requires you to look for new people to join your primary circle, which we will discuss in the next chapter. If you start out with even a few strong links in your primary circle, you'll create the basis for meaningful, fulfilling relationships that will yield the kind of transformational opportunities that are the result of Networlding.

CHAPTER FIVE

Step Three: Expand Your Circles

It would be great if we could form our networld only from existing relationships, because it would save us a significant amount of work. Unfortunately, the people we know don't always qualify as Networlding partners. Their values don't match ours or they lack the qualities essential for networlders. Although some of you may have created a good list of potential Networlding candidates during Step Two, in the previous chapter, many of you probably found only a few solid possibilities. That's fine—one networlder is worth more than her weight in contacts—but you may need to go outside your circle of friends, family, and business connections to complete your primary circle.

If you think of this process in networking terms—working a room, exchanging business cards, knocking on doors—you may feel everything from intimidation to boredom. But going out Networlding is a completely different experience, and a much more fulfilling one. You're looking not for mercenary contacts but for mutual connections, someone who will share and listen, with whom you'll exchange goals and dreams. You're not stumbling around blindly but taking highly conscious steps toward individuals who will be just as excited about meeting you as you are about meeting them. Together you can enjoy deeper, richer lives in which you build wisdom and opportunities.

We're inviting you to become the architect of your networld and find people who share similar values and will help you create a primary circle to support what you wish to have in your life. To do so, we'd like you to think of this primary circle as your first circle of influence. Through it, you'll gather the influence necessary to reach your goals. You'll also create secondary and tertiary circles of influence. Although these circles are less important than your primary one, they are still significant. All your circles are dynamic, and as circumstances change in your life and new opportunities arise someone in your secondary or tertiary circle could move quickly into your primary circle (while people in your primary circle may move into the secondary or tertiary ones). Back-and-forth movements between circles are not like promotions or demotions. The people in all three circles are networlders who will be in different positions to partner with you at different points in your life as well as theirs.

How to Choose Your Circles

Your primary circle is made up of the people you interact with most frequently. They are like a combination personal think tank and pit team, offering encouragement, information, and ideas in achieving what is most important to you. They are the foundation on which your networld is built, and so they must be selected carefully.

As we said in Chapter Two, limit yourself to no more than ten people. Trying to develop and leverage a group larger than ten is very difficult, both from time and relationship standpoints. We have found that many successful people have only three, four, or five people in their inner group. Secondary and tertiary circles, in contrast, can be unlimited in number because they don't demand the same level of time or involvement as a primary circle.

Fill Your Primary Circle with Influencers

In developing your primary circle, choose members who have the traits of networlders, share your values, and are influencers. Influencers are people who have the ability to influence other people and their actions. The first two criteria we've already discussed in detail. But the concept of influencers was only touched upon. It's especially important here because these are the type of people you need to seek when making connections. If you're like most individuals we work with, your current list of connections has few if any influencers on it. Influential people *seem to be* out of reach for those of us who aren't part of the elite in our respective industries. In fact, they are within reach for all of us if we learn how to reach them.

Before explaining how to do so, we'd like you to try an exercise that will prepare you to search for new networld partners. Close your eyes and imagine the primary circle that you're going to develop. Reflect on your values as well as the people and traits we examined in the previous chapter. Don't place any restrictions on your primary circle. It doesn't matter if you have an entry-level job or if you're out of work. Simply imagine the ideal mix of people who possess the knowledge, skills, ideas, and connections that would make your circle complete. Write all this on a piece of paper. The writing process will bring clarity to your thinking and help you envision what you're looking for so you'll know it when you see it.

We'd also like you to prepare yourself for some possible relationship changes. As you find individuals who are well suited to your primary circle, you may no longer view your current list of contacts in the same light. You may realize that some of them don't hold the same values as you or don't possess the traits you've come to esteem. Or it may simply be that you have to make choices about the people you're going to spend the most time with, and you prefer some of the new connections to the old contacts. But you probably will also be surprised to find that current relationships will deepen, and people with whom you have enjoyed a pleasant connection will become indispensable members of your primary circle. We're introducing you to a powerful process, and we know from experience that it can have a transforming impact on relationships. Go forward knowing that it will be enormously rewarding and fulfilling.

What Exactly Is an Influencer?

Let's expand again what we mean by influence. We define it as the power to affect another person, people, or course of events. Although position and wealth certainly confer influence, we've found that networlders also have *earned influence*: that is, they've achieved their power to influence based on a particular set of skills, knowledge, and accomplishments. In a networld, influence is a mutual quality; both partners use their "power to affect" to help each other accomplish important goals.

Influence is not a passive or title-based concept, at least in the networld sense. Just because someone is a CEO in your industry or has accumulated a great deal of wealth doesn't mean he or she has influence. Influencers are doers, not observers. They will act on your behalf rather than just talk a good game. Someone who has made his fortune or achieved his title may once have been an influencer but now has essentially retired from that influential state. It's very easy in our society to be impressed by titles, but there are influential people out there who don't hold prestigious titles. For instance, an administrative assistant who shares your values and possesses many Networlding traits may be a far better member of your circle than someone of visible power and authority. The administrative assistant may be able to influence events through her innovative ideas and sound suggestions; she may be connected to other influencers through her job, family, or friends. People listen to her ideas. They trust her judgment. When she recommends other people and their ideas, others act on those recommendations.

An example of an administrative influencer is Jan, who works for a prestigious literary agency. When Steven had difficulty getting his latest book proposal looked at by an agent he had selected from a writer's guide to literary agents, he called the agency. Jan, the administrative assistant to the agent, was clearly a good gatekeeper. Steven developed a rapport with her as he explored, in short conversations each time he called, what mattered most to her. He found she loved gardening, and in small but sincere ways he engaged her in conversation about gardens. He soon found himself in front of the agent who was originally impossible to reach. Therefore, keep an open mind about who influencers might be, and look for sincere ways to connect with them.

Furthermore, there are influencers and then there are influencers. Influence is a loaded term and may conjure up people who are antithetical to Networlding. In our view, people are mistakenly seen as influential just because they wield great power. Dictators like Mu'ammar Gadhafi and Saddam Hussein are powerful without being influential; their impact comes from brute force rather than knowledge, ideas, empathy, and the like. Similarly, someone may be considered a leader in an industry but is selfish and unreliable. That person may indeed have a certain amount of influence in one sense of the term, but it's a hollow, short-term influence because no one trusts or believes in her. She might make a pronouncement about a coming trend, but there's immediate distrust about the pronouncement because people assume she's speaking out of self-interest.

For these reasons, we'd like to clarify our definition of influence. Specifically, we'd like to talk about six behaviors manifested by influential networlders. These behaviors may not be what first comes to mind when you think of influential people (just as some of the Networlding traits described in the previous chapter aren't what come to mind when you think of networkers). These six behaviors will give you a better sense of what we mean.

Willingness to Give

Influencers enjoy helping others build their businesses and are extraordinarily generous with their time and resources. They establish reputations for giving rather than taking, and as a result everyone wants them on their team. Their influence is a direct result of how much they contribute to others; their impact stems from their willingness to share knowledge, ideas, and information that can create opportunities.

One influencer who exemplifies this quality is Pat Biedar. Pat is the owner of a sheet metal fabricating shop in Elk Grove Village, Illinois. Through hard work and perseverance over the past fifteen years, she has converted what was a company with severe financial problems into a multimillion dollar enterprise. Pat loves to help entrepreneurs. She constantly takes young entrepreneurs under her wing, introducing them at chamber of commerce gatherings and other association meetings. She plays business matchmaker, locating in her networld other people she knows who may need what her networld source has to sell. She humbly says she has had so many people who have helped her become more successful that she wants to do something in return. Pat has a profound impact both as a mentor and as a creator of business opportunities.

Community Involvement

This is one of the most important traits for a networlder and an influencer. Community involvement is a tremendous way to establish new and significant relationships. Influencers can build a diverse group of connections through community activities, gaining introductions to people from virtually every walk of life (rather than just people in their own profession). In addition, the impulse to be involved in community activities is a signal that someone is willing to work for the good of a group or a cause rather than just himself or herself. These people realize that community improvement means their lives improve too, but more important they have a deep passion to serve. You can find many of these influencers working on committees for local organizations. They will be written about in your local and national newspapers and magazines. It is often mind-boggling to see the many activities in which these people are involved. Andrea, for example, is the owner of a five-year-old marketing firm but she's also a member of a very successful and active children's organization and has recently started a home-based business group. She spends the time supporting this organization because she knows she can be influential in making a big improvement in her community. In other words, she realizes she can *make a difference*.

Awareness of Others' Needs and Interests

Influencers have an uncanny ability to anticipate and respond to other people's concerns. It's almost as if they can read a person's mind and say or do what is exactly right. Their influence stems in part from their ability to be proactive; they can act first and fast because they've made an effort to know what the other person wants. The most influential salespeople, for instance, are often the ones who are keenly aware of what their customers' product and service requirements are. The same is true for all service professionals—doctor, lawyer, banker—who are able to shut down their egos and truly listen and learn about their clients. There is an almost magical aura that surrounds highly aware people, and they're the ones people are willing to trust.

Influencers make great Networlding partners because they're terrific at knowing what your Networlding needs are. Their awareness translates into introducing you to just the right people at just the right time.

Dependability

Unreliable individuals tend to have little influence; they seem fickle, irresponsible, and untrustworthy. Dependable people come through for you. They show up on time and deliver on their promises. There are no surprises. They are rock solid, and their presence in a business deal is reassuring to everyone. As a result, everyone wants to deal with them because they know they can count on them.

Persistence

To paraphrase the old saying, influence is as much perspiration as inspiration. People who make an impact are the people who don't give up. You can make a long list of the politicians who were defeated time and after time but continued to pursue elective office with dogged persistence. Persistence pays off in many ways, not the least of which is that it demonstrates how serious someone is about an issue. This persistence earns everyone's respect. You can trust that these people will stick with you in good times and bad, and the sheer determination they bring to emerging opportunities serves networlders well.

Covisioning

What we mean by covisioning is a willingness to blend one's vision with someone else's rather than insisting on a singular vision of how things should be. In many respects, the solo visionary is a symbol of the networking past. The rugged individualism with which old-time entrepreneurs pursued their ideas was admirable, but it also meant that they didn't listen well (or at all) to others or develop synergistic strategies. The most influential people we know—CEOs, not-for-profit leaders, community activists, Internet innovators—are those who exhibit what we call covisioning behaviors.

For example, several years ago while writing her first book, Melissa developed a relationship with Sam McGrier, the regional director of the Small Business Administration (SBA) in her area. He knew that her vision was to be a small business advocate, which she accomplished through special entrepreneurial training scholarships for disadvantaged individuals. Sam also had a vision that was similar but not identical, and he shared his small business advocacy ideas with Melissa. Together, they began working at covisioning. The result was that Sam contacted Melissa every time he knew there was an SBA grant available for teaching entrepreneurs.

Through his support and direction, she was able to obtain a development grant to teach a course on networking for entrepreneurs. In turn, Melissa has worked as a volunteer for several SBA conferences in which Sam was involved.

How to Identify an Influencer

Influencers aren't easily identified by their behaviors. After all, there are many giving, community-minded, dependable people in the world who have very little influence; they simply don't make an impact despite all their good qualities. Impact comes from a few attributes, and influencers have at least one of them in spades. We'd like to discuss each one in some detail so you know what "assets" you're looking for in the people you meet:

Broad Base of Knowledge

They say that knowledge is power, and we say that the broader the base of the knowledge, the more influential someone can be. By broad base of knowledge, we mean knowledge of an unusually wide range of information. Most people are experts in a very narrow field (usually related to what they do, day in and day out). But the knowledge of some people crosses boundaries, such as a doctor who is well-versed in alternative medicine as well as his medical specialty or an environmental law expert who is also aware of a variety of tangential issues from endangered species to ecological problems.

Influencers leverage their broad base of knowledge in many ways. Most obviously, they use it to come up with innovative ideas. Their advantage is that they're drawing on a more diverse body of knowledge than other people, and their ideas reflect that. They don't volunteer the same tired concepts as everyone else. As a result, their knowledge has an impact. Of course, some people with a broad base of knowledge may not make an impact. A librarian or a scholar who just "sits" on that knowledge doesn't affect the world. As we mentioned earlier, influencers are doers; they do something with their broad base of knowledge.

David Raccuglia, the creator and founder of American Crew, the high-quality men's grooming product line sold in many national and international hair salons, is a true networlder who has used his knowledge well. Trained as a barber, David branched out and became extraordinarily informed about the fashion and grooming industries. Even early in his career, this knowledge paid off when he was hired by a London firm to train hairstylists around the world in the latest techniques. David became what is called a *featured platform artist*. While still in his twenties, he was consultant to a large chain of salons and several national product companies that recognized his knowledge and influence. At this point, his skills were no longer limited to the fashion and hairstyling industries but included a number of business skills as well, like public relations.

When he was in his early thirties, David and his wife decided to settle down, buy a home, and open a salon with another couple. The salon, Art + Science, in Evanston, Illinois, quickly became one of the most respected and influential in the area and was featured in local and national publications like *The Chicago Tribune, North Shore, Vogue,* and *Self.* David's base of knowledge was broad enough that he understood the importance of sending fashion and grooming ideas and high-quality professional photographs of hairstyles to industry and consumer media journalists. He was also astute about maintaining international fashion contacts, recognizing that international events could have a local payoff. He was able to parlay his understanding of the international fashion scene into a cover story and photo spread on fashion in the Soviet Union for *American Salon* magazine, which resulted in a great deal of positive publicity for his salon. Just as important, David had good communication skills and was well-versed in psychological principles; he understood that most salons fail to communicate well with their customers and don't recognize which ambiance would make intelligent professionals feel comfortable. David created an unusual training regimen for his stylists, sharing his expertise and making sure they knew how to communicate with their customers.

The story of David and his product line is such a great Networlding story that we are using it to demonstrate many of the ideas articulated throughout this book—things we have experienced and observed throughout our professional careers in business. David was already successful in two previous business enterprises and created his product line out of his belief that it is important to make a difference. The motivation to develop the products drew from treasured memories from his childhood; going to the barbershop with his dad, the ritual of sitting in the chair, the towels, the utensils, the conversations, the astringents and powders, and the smells were all part of special times in the experience of being a male. At the time he created American Crew, he felt that most men were lost in a kind of limbo: barbershops were now passé, out of date with current fashion trends, and scores were closing their doors. Yet most salons were too weird, too feminine for men. David felt that men deserved their own modern grooming rituals and products, just as women had theirs.

David was ingenious in his launch of American Crew in the mid-1990s. Once he was satisfied that his product line was excellent, he decided to use his broad industry knowledge and perspective, high span of influence, positive public perception, large support base, activity in industry organizations, and skills of influence to create an innovative marketing campaign that generated extremely positive word of mouth and involved no paid advertising media.

David created local and national industry hair shows, featuring the latest in hairstyling techniques for men, very similar in nature to those he appeared at as a guest educator, and for which he had respect. Stylists paid for tickets to the events, just as they did for other educational events, covering some of the production costs. Stylists attended to learn new techniques useful to them in their professions, to learn about the product line (which was positioned as key to achieving these new styles), to be treated to a high-quality, entertaining event with professional and amateur models and music, and to receive complimentary full-size samples of the products: a shampoo, conditioner, several styling gels, and a water-based pomade (the first of its kind ever). The products were also positioned as excellent tools for increasing each salon's male clientele. Stylists were advised to dedicate a window to an appealing, professional American Crew poster and product display, to demonstrate to passers-by and current clients that this was a male-friendly salon.

It worked. Stylists couldn't wait to return to the salons and try out the new skills and new products. The products *were* different, superior to any on the market. In fact, they were soon beloved by stylists and consumers. Even women used some of the products, and people talked about them to their friends. Although David invested in a public relations campaign, many articles appeared in various newspapers without any effort on the part of David's firm, generated by overwhelmingly positive public word of mouth. David continued with his strategy, producing shows throughout the United States in major as well as smaller cities, and private demonstrations at important salons. He created brochures featuring professional models and the rowing team at Cornell University. These photo shoots became the basis for the posters used in the various salons. He offered American Crew seminars on marketing to men.

In just over a year after the launch, David was approached by Revlon. They saw the potential for the firm and the product line and saw what American Crew was able to create in such a short period of time with minimal marketing investment. Revlon purchased his firm, paying David a very good price, and asked him to continue working with them as a consultant. The company continues to grow internationally, using the same basic marketing strategy David developed. He has now worked with Revlon to develop other product lines.

Throughout the years, David developed many relationships throughout the industry; the connections and the identity he built were instrumental to the success of his company. David is a masterful Networlding influencer.

David could never have accomplished what he has if he had been content with knowledge of hairstyling. By broadening his knowledge base, he became tremendously influential. He is a great contributor of ideas and connections to those fortunate enough to be in his networld.

> *Action step:* When you meet people, consider whether they possess an extensive body of knowledge. Be alert for clear conversational signs, like an ability to talk easily about a wide range of subjects or a tremendous command of many areas of a given industry or profession. You're going to have to listen carefully to differentiate bombast from true knowledge. Some people are facile talkers, but if you ask them a few probing questions you will be able to determine if their knowledge base is broad or shallow. If they respond with evasive or general answers, the odds are they lack the body of knowledge influencers usually have.

Large Perspective

Some people see things as they are; others see things as they might be. The ability to see things others don't is a gift that many influencers possess. A large perspective can relate to the present or the future. Some influencers are visionaries whereas others can look at current complexities and place them in an understandable and usable context. A large perspective reveals everything from immediate opportunities and connections you might have overlooked to emerging trends.

In one sense, a large perspective can be translated into "eye-opening insights." For example, Deepak Chopra has made an industry out of his large perspective. Now a well-known author and speaker, the former chief of staff of New England Memorial Hospital has utilized his broad base of knowledge as a Western-trained endocrinologist and a student of ancient Indian Ayurvedic medicine as well as his large perspective to identify and promote the connection between the mind and body.

Of course, having a large perspective can be on a smaller scale than going so far as to create a hybrid field of medicine. For example, you might meet a colleague who has an uncanny ability to create business strategies that are more forward-thinking and far-reaching than any you've encountered previously. You might discover that rare accountant who can break out of the standard CPA thinking mode and see new and cost-effective ways for you to structure your business. Or you might encounter a consultant who identifies trends and markets that no consultant ever identified before.

A large perspective may not always be right on the money, but it gets everyone thinking in fresh directions. You want someone who can stimulate fresh thinking in your netword if only because those thoughts can have a significant influence on your career direction as well as your business opportunities.

Action step: Be conscious of people who surprise you with their insights and observations. Note statements that indicate an ability to envision a different type of future or a skill at synthesizing diverse facts into a coherent whole. At the very least, jot down the names of people you meet who have "interesting" perspectives, who view the world in a different light than most.

Difference-Makers

This is an attribute that we'd advise you to evaluate with care. The people who are difference-makers are usually people who have attained "high office." They're elected officials, executive directors of associations, senior business executives, celebrities, well-regarded academics, and the like. But as we pointed out earlier, simply holding a prestigious title or job doesn't mean a person is a true influencer. People who use their difference-making platforms for others are the influencers you should watch for. They're the ones who exercise their influence to help people grow in their careers, create mutually beneficial opportunities, and create connections, alliances, and other collaborative relationships.

We've found that the majority of difference-makers qualify as influencers. They're giving, caring people who are concerned about helping others and making a difference in their lives. Thus, meeting difference-makers, whether in government or in private industry, is not as difficult as it looks. If approached with respect and sincerity, most will respond positively. Furthermore, these influencers not only have superior connections because of their positions but also access to valuable information and resources. Over the years, we've seen many of these difference-makers mentor others, help them secure capital for ventures, and lend their names and time to joint ventures.

Lester Blair, a money manager who founded his own firm, Blair Capital Management Corporation, had long-term dreams of running for public office. Blair decided to attempt to develop a relationship with Dick Durbin, who at the time was running for his first term as U.S. Senator of Illinois. After introducing himself to the candidate, Blair was invited to become involved in fundraising for Senator Durbin's campaign. Because he has many clients and contacts in the African-American community, Blair helped Senator Durbin broaden his base in that community, and eventually the senator won the election. In turn, Senator Durbin is an excellent connection for Blair. Although he is not in Blair's primary circle, he is in his secondary one and because of the dynamics of networld circles, he may join the primary group at some point in the future.

It would be a mistake to create a primary circle composed only of difference-makers—you need a more balanced set of assets—but you should look for at least one person with this attribute.

Action step: Create a wish list of people you might contact who are highly visible in your community or industry. Don't be intimidated by who they are or their seeming inaccessibility. Instead, determine if their goals and values are aligned with your own based on what you've heard or read about them. Do they manifest the traits of networlders and the behaviors of influencers? If so, try to contact them. If they hold political office, one entry point might be as a volunteer for their political organization. If they are top executives, write them a letter or send them an e-mail demonstrating that you are in synch with their values and goals and suggest a meeting or phone conference to exchange ideas. Of course, it is difficult to arrange meetings or even phone conversations with people as famous as Steven Spielberg, Oprah Winfrey, Bill Gates, and other megacelebrities, but just about everyone else is more accessible than you might think.

Norma used this tactic to reach thought leaders in her industry. As a trainer in the area of sales and marketing, she was always reading about gurus in her field, such as Seth Godin, author of *Permission Marketing*. She found that she was able to start Networlding exchanges with these leaders by reading their latest works and then visiting their Web sites, where she could e-mail them. Today, Norma finds herself exchanging ideas and getting endorsements for her training materials with one or two thought leaders monthly.

Active in Organizations

Influencers are frequently involved in a variety of trade associations, community groups, not-for-profit organizations, think tanks, and so on. Some are on the boards of these groups, others are simply members. All have established relationships among organization members—relationships that might serve you well. These influencers aren't always difference-makers with prestigious titles, but they are definitely doers. They become involved and contribute, and their level of activity carries weight with people, as do the variety of relationships they've established. In other words, they are very involved in diverse community caregiving activities and gain influence as a result. Examples here are the active volunteers who are involved in a variety of charitable organizations. Rather than focus all their organizational work in one arena (that is, the company they work for), they've branched out into at least one other area. This gives them access to people and knowledge they might not ordinarily have.

Jerry, for instance, is an ad agency executive who is very active in a charitable organization composed of people from the advertising and marketing fields. For over ten years, he has thrown himself into this charitable work so fully that he was elected president of the charity. Jerry is dedicated to the goals of the charity—helping needy children—but his participation has also led to relationships with some brilliant marketers and advertising executives. He has so many high-powered connections and is privy to so much industry scuttlebutt that both media people and agency friends routinely call him to confirm or deny rumors. Jerry is more tuned in to what's happening in his field than just about anyone, and he's helped many people find jobs. Jerry is also held in great respect by many top people, not only for what and who he knows but for his dedication to a charitable cause.

> *Action step:* What we suggest here is actually a two-step process. First, think about a group you'd like to join, one that truly interests you and does things you believe to be worthwhile. It doesn't have to be a trade association in your field. It can be the Boy Scouts, a committee that supervises a soccer league for girls, an ecology group, or any other organization that appeals to you. Second, determine if there is a member of the group who has one or another quality of a Networlding influencer. If there is, it makes sense to join the group and attempt to make this person's acquaintance. You should not join the group, however, solely to meet someone. You need to believe in what the group stands for.

Skilled Communicators

Some people derive their influence from their great ability to communicate. These people include speakers, public relations and advertising professionals, communications consultants, and members of the media. If you lack communications skills or your level of skill is merely adequate, you may want to consider someone like this for your networld. Again, we're not suggesting that any reporter or public relations professional is suitable to include in your networld. You need to screen everyone through the criteria we've established. If they seem like good candidates, however, you probably have skills and knowledge that you can exchange with them so that an alliance would be mutually beneficial.

To a certain extent, the type of skilled communicator appropriate for your networld depends on your goals. If you want to become an author and speaker, you probably should consider a writer and speaking bureau head for your primary network. If you intend to run for public office, you might want to align yourself with an image consultant or someone who specializes in political marketing.

> *Action step:* The easy thing to do here is to determine what communication skills you both need and lack, and then create a list of people in your area who possess these skills. For instance, if advertising skills are important for achieving your goals, create a list of ad agency presidents or executives in your town (or in another city if there are none in your vicinity).

Reaching Influencers

As we described the assets of influencers, we offered some suggestions about how you might identify them and even find a place or situation where you'd be likely to encounter them. Influencers are not a rare species. In fact, you'll find them everywhere. They are leading organizations, writing trade journal articles, organizing your community, participating in your chamber of commerce, becoming leaders of charities and other not-for-profit associations, and speaking at events. The steps you take in finding influencers will be guided in large part by what you wish to accomplish and who you feel would make a great member of your network.

As an informational step, it makes sense to read a lot. This might not be essential for those of you who have a good sense of the influencers you want to contact but still, it's astonishing how many viable influencers you can uncover if you read a variety of publications on a regular basis. The most obvious magazines to peruse are those that cover your particular industry. But it also makes sense to read general-interest publications and newspapers with an eye toward your goals, while keeping in mind the traits and assets of influencers. This will help you not only recognize the leaders in your field but other leaders as well—everyone from community leaders to those in other fields. Influencers know other influencers, and one will lead you to another. Therefore, it helps you to know who these people are. Reading will also inform you about the trends in your area of interest. After all, when you meet an influencer, you need to be able to talk intelligently about your mutual interests.

Communicating your values is another indirect method that will bring you in contact with influencers. When you make your values known, it sometimes sets forth a chain of events that brings an influencer into your life. Mario, a commercial real estate broker, was looking for influencers in real estate who valued building commercial properties that were environmentally sound. Mario had made this value clear to Thalia, a woman with whom he had worked in the past. She in turn introduced him to Jane, who was a leader in building so-called ecocommunities. Jane and Mario met, and Jane resonated with Mario's values. She brought him in to work on a real estate project in a large city that eventually helped revitalize a blighted area. Jane and Mario are now working together on even more ambitious ecocommunities. If Mario had never communicated his values to Thalia, however, he would never have met this particular influencer.

Another example comes from a conference we recently attended. There was a speaker who headed a Fortune 1000 company, whose topic was mentoring. She shared a story about a relationship she had had with a young woman over the past decade. She said she never thought of the professional friendship they had as a mentoring relationship until the young woman said to her, "Thank you for being my mentor all these years." The speaker shared with us her reply: if she had known she was seen as a mentor, she believed she would have done even more for her younger protégée. We now encourage all those whom we meet to articulate to potential networld partners, if appropriate, that they are seeking a mentoring relationship. We have since discovered it is very effective in creating powerful relationships that yield benefits for both participants.

Written as well as verbal communication can help you meet influencers. When you see an influencer who has written an article or been written about, send that person a copy of the article with your congratulations. Let him or her know that you are out there and admire good work. And of course, communicate your values in any written correspondence. Although it's great if you have shared interests, knowledge, or skills that you think might help an influencer, a value statement can really grab someone's attention if their values are compatible.

It's also useful to keep in mind that you can use your own influence to attract an influencer. If you're just starting out in your career or don't have a high-level position, you may ask, "My influence?" Yet, we all can place ourselves in positions where we have a measure of influence. For instance, there are often opportunities for all levels of people to work on program committees of industry associations. If you volunteer, you may find yourself in charge of locating industry leaders who would be interested in speaking at an association conference. You can have an influence on which individual is chosen to speak; you can make a recommendation based on your interviews with potential speakers. Through this communication and by your choice of someone who you feel is a potential networlder, you may find yourself helping an influencer achieve a goal. In this way, you will have made a connection with someone you may want to include in your primary circle.

Pathways to Finding Influencers

Though some of you may still be skeptical about your ability to find influencers and establish Networlding relationships with them, we can assure you that if you just follow the previous suggestions you're likely to bring them into your life. But you can also do more. You can be proactive and highly conscious in your search for influencers and accelerate the process. Here are some pathways to pursue that may lead to networld relationships with these individuals.

Through the Internet

Simply entering key words using a search engine can lead you to experts in any industry you choose; they will direct you to Web sites that encourage connections. Once you've identified an influencer at a site look for something that this individual has "said" that touches you emotionally as well as intellectually. E-mail the person to support those ideas. If you present yourself genuinely and specifically point out things you appreciate about him or her, this influencer may well respond in kind. The Internet is a more responsive communication medium than any other, at least in the sense that it's so easy to express ideas quickly and directly there. Many of the social barriers to communication that exist in other mediums are absent on the Internet. Cyberspace is an environment of inherent equality (it's difficult to judge someone you can't see or hear) where people establish relationships based on the words they type. It is therefore a great opportunity to reach someone because an influencer will treat you as an equal and you are less likely to be intimidated by that person's reputation (as you might be if you met in person). In addition, the Internet helps you cross geographic boundaries to meet influencers. You may live in a small town, but suddenly you have access to an influencer in a big city. Or you may need to establish a relationship with someone in another country. The Internet will provide you with unprecedented access to all types of influencers. One good site to explore is the Fast Company site; another is guru.com. Many influencers showcased on these sites share their passions through compelling stories. David Neals, the head of telementoring at Hewlett-Packard, and Chris Turner, who used to be a knowledge manager at Xerox and has coauthored the book *All Hat and No Cattle,* are just two of the people we have met through on-line exchanges. The Fast Company site offers on-line articles from its monthly magazine, which focuses on leading-edge and bleeding-edge companies and thought leaders. Guru.com is a portal for thought leaders in almost every industry.

Through Periodicals

We've emphasized how reading all sorts of publications can help you become aware of influencers. Let's now look at what you can do when you come across a potential networlder in an article.

Because e-mail addresses are sometimes included at the end of articles, you can once again take advantage of the Internet to provide feedback to article writers on their subjects immediately. Even if an e-mail address isn't listed, you can contact the individual the old-fashioned way—through a phone call or letter. Again, communicate honestly and emotionally. Explain your interest in the concepts the writer expressed. Express your values and how they dovetail with the ideas of the influencer.

Local newspapers are especially useful in locating influencers because the people interviewed are often geographically accessible. This increases the chances that you can meet the influencer in person. When you contact them and request a meeting, don't communicate as if you're writing a fan letter. In all communication with influencers, remember that you're not attempting to establish a subservient relationship. You have something to offer the influencer; *mutually* beneficial relationships are crucial to Networlding. In your correspondence with the influencer, suggest what it is you might be able to contribute. As you'll recall, this doesn't have to be something monumental like an opportunity to make a million dollars. It can be an idea, information, connections to people you know, promotional support, and so on.

The op-ed page or editorial viewpoint columns are great places to look for influencers. Generally, people of influence in a given industry or community use these forums to express deeply felt opinions that reflect their values as well. Your response to these essays will often elicit a positive response from influencers.

Through Conferences and Lectures

When you attend conferences, do you introduce yourself to the speakers? If you don't, you are missing out on a wonderful opportunity to meet new Networlding partners. Let's say you attend a conference where the speaker is talking about new ways of working through intranets. You find the ideas engaging and compelling. We suggest that you write a question related to the talk on the back of your card, and approach the speaker afterward. Next, talk with the speaker, telling him that you enjoyed his speech and that you wrote down a question you would like to discuss with him for five minutes sometime in the next two weeks. In this way, you will show that you are aware that he has a busy schedule by having prepared ahead of time. Ask for his business card, and if he has one, take it, thank him, and hand your card to him. If he doesn't have a card ask what is the best way to get in contact with him or if he has a Web site where information is posted. (Most industry influencers now have their own sites.)

Follow up with the speaker in a few days and ask when you can call him to talk for five minutes. When you call, be sure to keep it to the five minutes you promised. This is very important because you're demonstrating not only the ability to keep your word but also a recognition that the influencer's time is valuable. In the coming weeks or months when you notice articles featuring the speaker or learn of information you know would be of interest to him, send it along with a note. If you happen to discover an opportunity that you think might interest him, pass it on. In this way, you will establish a foundation for a possible Networlding relationship. You are also setting the pattern for an ongoing value exchange. If the influencer responds in kind—if he demonstrates a willingness to share information, ideas, and opportunities with you—then you've achieved your objective. By thoughtfully preparing and offering value during each connection, you set into action similar behavior.

This pathway is especially valuable for networlders, because nothing beats personal interaction as a relationship's starting point. After hearing someone speak, you have a small but real window of opportunity to establish a connection. The speaker is open to feedback from his audience, so it's your job to give it quickly and sincerely.

Through Volunteering

As we emphasized earlier, volunteering is a terrific way to come in contact with influencers. It's important, however, not to volunteer either randomly or in a calculating manner. Volunteering pays off in connections when it's done from the heart rather than the head. Look for groups that espouse your beliefs or whose goals and values mirror your own. Whether it's volunteering to work for a political candidate you believe in or raising money for a charity that's fighting a disease that's affected your family, make sure it's something that is consistent with your values.

Volunteering for these groups will not only give you a great opportunity to make your values known but also expose you to influencers from all walks of life. We've found that some influencers put as much if not more energy into their volunteer efforts as their regular jobs. Many have made significant sums of money and are set for life; now they've turned their attention to other matters that are more meaningful to them. Thus, if you can establish a connection at the volunteer level, it will be strong and meaningful to the influencer.

In volunteer work, simply be aware of who's working with you on a given fundraising project or on other activity. When you find an influencer, strike up a conversation about the work you are doing. Use that common purpose as a starting point for a relationship and see what develops.

Through Program Committees

Most industry associations and other special interest groups that you can join have program committees that are responsible for booking speakers. If you are on that committee, connecting to industry influencers will be part of your job. Being on these committees gives you the opportunity to contact an influencer as well as the chance to use your own influence on his or her behalf. That's just what Joe did. He took responsibility for locating more than half the speakers at his software association's national conference—speakers who were all very successful leaders in the high-tech area. Joe built strong professional friendships with some of the speakers and five years later still networlds with them. It didn't matter that he was a start-up entrepreneur with very little money in the bank. He was able to leverage his position in the software association and add value by providing a specific opportunity for these speakers.

Through Lists, Directories, Alumni Groups

You can locate influencers through lists, and your alumni directory is a good place to start. Check with your alma mater to find what on-line alumni directory they have and then get involved by participating in their on-line community. Reunite with past friends and fellow classmates and be alert for those who have become influencers. Because you went to school with these people, you have a natural bond. It's possible that this bond isn't important to that individual, or he may lack the values and traits of a networlder. Nevertheless, this is a way to make connections that you shouldn't dismiss. Also look over other lists such as "Who's Who" directories, Internet provider membership listings (such as that of America Online), and other published documents that contain names and numbers of people you knew in the past and can contact.

As you survey the lists that interest you, look for *patterns*. For instance, you see the name *Mary Smith* in your college alumni directory. You remember that you and Mary worked on the college newspaper together. You enter her name on an Internet search engine and find that she's now one of the top editors at a women's fashion magazine. Meanwhile, you now work for a large public relations agency, and some of your agency's accounts include companies in clothing manufacturing industry. You're not sure if there's a fit, but there is definitely a pattern. It's therefore worth getting in touch with Mary Smith to see if she's good Networlding material and to explore getting together.

When Traveling

Helen makes it a habit to fly first class whenever possible. She has met an ambassador to Switzerland, a vice president of a leading Fortune 500 company, and a number of best-selling authors. She finds that most of these people are very open and interested in talking with her. As a management consultant she has learned that exchanges with influencers on airplanes lead to Networlding relationships that in turn translate into new projects. She cautions that anyone wishing to networld in this way be very sensitive to a seat partner's desire to be left alone.

You can test their sensitivity simply by making an innocuous remark about the airline food, turbulence, or the weather. If someone responds curtly (or not at all), don't pursue the conversation. However, if you receive an encouraging, friendly response, ratchet up the conversation to the next level (asking about what is bringing them to the city you're traveling to, for instance). If your seat partner remains receptive, push the conversation forward and to more important subjects.

Airline travel is a great leveler in a different way from the Internet. When you're trapped in a cylinder hurtling across a country at great speeds, everyone is reduced to a very vulnerable state. Sometimes, this helps influencers open up when they might not do so as readily in other situations. Furthermore, airline travel can be boring, especially if there have been numerous delays. To relieve the boredom, people are often open to conversation.

Through Leisure Activities

Be open to developing Networlding relationships everywhere. Your sailing class, cooking class, bicycling team, and rollerblading groups may include potential networlders. People are sometimes under the mistaken notion that you can only meet influencers in work-related situations. In reality, fun situations are often even more fertile ground for establishing relationships. People are less on guard and more open about who they are; they're not working under deadline or with a specific goal in mind.

Of course, the person in your cooking class may not be an influencer. You're going to have do a bit of probing to discover who that person is. She may, of course, become a good friend, and we certainly can never have too many. What we're advocating, though, is meeting people who can fill both roles, primary circle partners and great friends. With this networld, over time you will co-create the kind of transformational life that actually finds you getting better and better results with less effort. But any casual conversation will soon reveal a person's status. Therefore, if this person is an influencer, then you just need to discover if he or she is also a potential networlder.

Through People Who Know People You Know

As we discussed in the previous chapter, everyone has hidden connections. For instance, when you meet John, you have no idea that he knows Betty, whom you've heard about but never met. Everyone has a web of connections that aren't apparent until you do some exploration. We assume that the people we know have relationships with a very small segment of the group they actually do know. Therefore, we never ask John for a referral to Betty.

There's a psychological principle that also prevents us from tapping into these hidden connections. What we call the *horizon of observability,* mentioned in Chapter Four, refers to our difficulty in seeing beyond our current connections. If you think of relationships as links on a chain, then we only see the link with whom we're directly connected. In reality, we're connected to many other links through the first one, but we don't see them because there's no direct connection.

It's unlikely that you're going to discover hidden connections inadvertently. You need to take action if you want to make invisible links visible. Taking action means establishing deeper relationships with people you do know. For example, when Sonya was completing her doctoral thesis in psychology she looked at all her career opportunities. Allison, the head of the placement office at Sonya's graduate school, was a nice person with whom she regularly had conversations. One day the two had a long conversation and Allison explained how she wanted to get her doctorate but was waiting until her children were older. This was something Allison didn't reveal to many people, but she sensed that Sonya would understand. When Sonya was empathic—her brother's wife had made the same decision—Allison also shared with Sonya her deep interest in and experience with art. Sonya responded that her sister, Erin, owned an art gallery and that she would probably be happy to look at Allison's art.

As they talked, Sonya revealed that although she had considered teaching once she received her doctorate, what she really wanted to do was open her own private practice. This was a difficult piece of information for Sonya to share, because the dean of the school frowned on graduates starting their own private practice without having worked at a hospital or done some other form of institutional work first. She was worried that Allison might caution her against this career route, but instead Allison told her that Carl, who had graduated five years earlier, was a good friend of hers and enjoyed a flourishing private practice. In fact, he had called Allison a few days before and said he was in great need of a junior partner. Allison suggested introducing Sonya to Carl. From that introduction Allison established a networld relationship with Carl that eventually (after she received her Ph.D.) turned into a business alliance. Carl, a brilliant psychologist who had become very influential in the field of child psychology, became Allison's mentor. It's useful to note that this conversation benefited Allison as well, because Sonya introduced her to Erin, who was impressed by her art and agreed to display her works in her gallery.

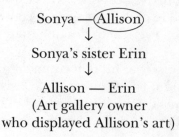

Sonya —(Allison)	Allison —(Sonya)
↓	↓
Sonya's sister Erin	Allison's friend Carl
↓	↓
Allison — Erin	Sonya — Carl
(Art gallery owner	(Psychologist who created
who displayed Allison's art)	a business alliance with Sonya)

Action step: What we suggested here. Think back to one relationship you've had that resulted in a great opportunity. Just as we did with Sonya and Allison, draw a diagram of the people who introduced you to this person who helped create this opportunity. Continue to work backward to see all the connections to this person.

Next, imagine a couple of scenarios as to how you might link to your current connections in building an opportunity you are now seeking. This exercise will help you stretch your horizon of observability and create what we call your "horizon of possibility"—those potential partners and opportunities.

Indeed, of all the pathways to influencers, this is the one that is most underutilized yet most likely to bear results. Sometimes all it takes to plug into these hidden connections is an in-depth conversation with someone you know and a willingness to share a significant piece of information about yourself: your career dreams, your values, your fears. In turn, the other person will respond by sharing something that's important to him or her. In the course of this sharing, you'll learn not only something about this individual that you didn't know but also that this person has people in his or her networld you may want to meet.

As you've probably realized, the way along this pathway is to share similar values. As Allison and Sonya demonstrated, a significant connection must be established before either person will grant access to their hidden connections. Here, you need to earn access, and you do that only by communicating your values and goals. Unlike in networking, the names you receive are usually more meaningful. Your current connection will be much more thoughtful about recommending someone for you to meet and thus will provide a much more compelling introduction.

All the people you know and have formed a bond with have at least one influencer among their hidden connections. In fact, we've found some people who have ten influencers or more. Many times, however, you're convinced that a current connection begins and ends with that individual. Networlders always take the optimistic and realistic point of view that there's an influencer linked to people they know well with whom they share similar interests and values.

Because most of us know a lot of people, it's difficult to know who to approach first and attempt to make their hidden connections visible. To give you a starting point, answer the following questions: Who do I know who is most likely to be linked to an influencer? Given this person's position, is it reasonable to assume he or she would know influential customers, suppliers, consultants, authors, speakers, or heads of organizations? Have I heard a friend, family member, or colleague talk about an individual in a way that made me think it would be worthwhile to get to know that person, that he or she possesses skills, interests, values, and ideas that dovetail with my own?

Combine Existing Connections with New Ones to Complete Your Primary Circle

In Step Two, in the last chapter, you identified potential networlders from a list of existing connections. Here you're qualifying and expanding that list based on fresh connections. Together, they will give you a primary circle of no more than ten people. Once again, make sure you have partners whose values are compatible and that they manifest the behaviors and attributes of a networlder. Also, as mentioned earlier, make sure all your partners have some ability to influence. Otherwise, these people should be placed in your secondary circles.

It's quite possible that you'll end up with too many names for too few slots in your primary circle. If this is the case, move some of them to your secondary and tertiary circles. Our emphasis on creating a primary circle is not about numbers. We're very sensitive to honoring all the relationships you have. Networlding is about giving you a better process to grow these relationships so that all parties involved experience joy and fulfillment. It's like being a good host at a party of great friends. You want everyone to enjoy themselves and want to return. Networlding at this step is about being that host who has taken the time to architect great possibility, joy, and adventure with like-minded, thoughtful people. The result of your effort will be making a difference for all those whose lives you touch. With Networlding, that could mean the whole world!

Envision and Create Your Secondary Circle

As we've emphasized throughout the book so far, networlds are dynamic. People move from primary to second to tertiary circles and back again over time. Just because you're assigning someone secondary status doesn't mean they will remain in that position forever. Practically speaking, your primary circle includes people who you interact with and feel more compatible with than people in your secondary circle. Use the following criteria to assign people to your secondary group:

- They have fewer values in common with you than people in your primary group.
- They possess goals that aren't completely aligned with your goals.
- They have areas of interests that don't match up perfectly with your own.
- They don't possess as many traits and behaviors of networlders as people in your primary group.
- They lack the time or interest to meet regularly or work together on many opportunities.

This last criterion is the most important, for you may have many commonalities with potential partners, but if they do not have the time or interest to covision opportunities, you are wasting your time (see Figure 5.1). In other words, it is a much more effective use of what planning time you have to create the continuous new opportunities you can develop in this new connected economy to be partnering with people who are, as we put it, "ready, willing, and able" to help. As you build your relationships through focused conversations in the process we call the exchange (which we will talk about more in the next chapter), you and your partners will accelerate both the richness of your relationship and the opportunities it generates. However, you need partners who understand the importance of taking time to covision and exchange.

Although you can cull some people for your secondary circle from those you originally considered for your primary one, you may also want to add some names, people you didn't consider before. Remember, you don't have to limit this second group to ten, so there's more margin for error. A good rule of thumb is to add diversity that may be missing from your primary circle (though ideally your primary group is also diverse). There may be some skills missing from your primary circle or it may be

Figure 5.1. Forming Networlding Circles.

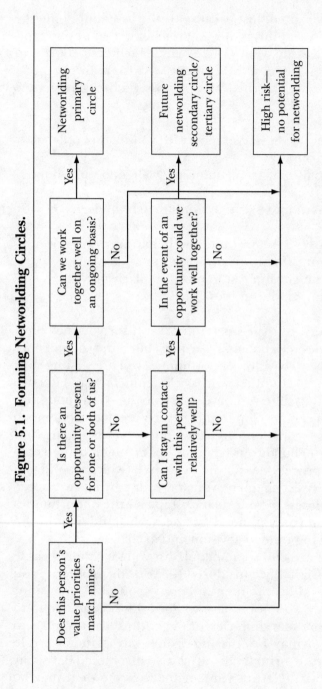

unbalanced in terms of age, sex, or ethnicity. This is an opportunity to fill in the gaps.

It's also possible that you initially thought some people seemed like networlders and influencers but you now question including them. A specific incident may have caused you to doubt their values, or a series of experiences may have made you wonder if your judgment was correct. This is not to say that you're rejecting them entirely or feel that you no longer want to have anything to do with them; it's just that you no longer feel quite as comfortable as you once did in your interactions. For instance, Carol realized that conversations with one of her oldest friends just weren't as rewarding or energizing as they once were. She would listen patiently to Daria's recent difficulties and ask if she would like suggestions. Daria would agree and listen, but over time Carol realized that Daria was increasingly focused on the problem rather than a solution. Although she still cared for her friend, Carol realized that she just didn't want to spend lengthy conversations each week on Daria's problems. There was no longer sufficient mutual support to justify Daria's inclusion in her primary circle. Carol remained in contact with Daria and continued to lend her support, but she wanted to devote more time to other relationships. As a result, she shifted her focus to other people but didn't rule out reestablishing her former primary relationship with Daria.

Develop a Picture of Your Tertiary Circle

Tertiary circles are wide, shallow, and full of weak contacts. Perhaps the best way to describe this third networld circle is *utilitarian*. The exchange here is often of services rather than something deeper. Typical exchanges with people in tertiary circles involve basic information of some type: job openings, data relating to trends, rumors about organizations, statistics, and so on.

This circle is a repository for people with Networlding potential as well as for those who provide useful information but may not be capable of providing anything more. The "potentials" may include influencers who have never demonstrated an inclination to share much beyond information but who definitely possess significant influence within certain spheres and may one day be willing to develop a more significant relationship with you. Others in the potential category are individuals who simply are so busy that they don't currently have time to devote to your relationship or are so young that they lack the maturity and experience necessary for a mutually beneficial partnership. The latter group consists of people who don't want anything more than informational relationships (at least at this time).

However, research has shown that tertiary relationships work very well when it comes to job hunting. Fellow alumni of your high school, college, or graduate programs are good candidates for connection.

In a sense, many of the people in your third Networlding circle are classic networkers. They may develop into true networlders in time, but right now they're best suited for a tertiary relationship.

Focus Your Time and Attention on Building Your Primary Circle

Figure 5.1 will help you determine which circle your Networlding partners belong in.

Your main task is to develop and deepen relationships with the people you've assigned to your primary circle. The ongoing exchanges and mutually beneficial support you will give one another will ensure more work and career opportunities as well as a more meaningful life. Take the following steps:

- Initiate contact (by phone, e-mail, fax, letter) with at least three people you consider prime candidates for your primary circle and who you've determined to be influencers.
- If the response is positive, schedule a meeting or lunch.
- If the meeting goes well, schedule additional meetings to exchange ideas, information, feelings, and opportunities.
- Tap into your networld partner's hidden connections.
- Continuously assess these three relationships to determine if they meet the criteria established for both networlders and influencers.
- Repeat these steps whenever possible to add to your primary circle and to replace any individual who no longer belongs in that circle—but don't exceed the maximum number of ten members.

Make and save a list of the names of the people you've designated for your secondary and tertiary circles. Stay aware of what the people in these circles are doing. Though you don't have to maintain regular contact, you should occasionally communicate with them with an eye toward determining if they're ready and willing to move into your primary circle, and assessing whether you can lend each other support from a skill or promotional standpoint. With those in your tertiary circle, keep the relationship on an informational basis. In addition to information exchanges, watch and see if someone with potential is changing his attitude or influence in ways that make him better suited to a secondary or primary circle. No matter which circle your Networlding partners belong to, your joint success will be based on your ability to initiate relationships with them in which meaningful exchanges occur for both of you.

CHAPTER SIX

Step Four: Initiate Exchanging Relationships

Whether you're attempting to establish Networlding relationships with people you know or with people you want to know, you need to take the initiative. Even basic networking isn't effective if you sit around hoping someone else will make contact. However, initiating Networlding relationships requires more than working a room and making phone calls. As we've already seen, the sine qua non of Networlding is a relationship exchange. Your objective is to establish relationships with mutual exchange as the foundation.

The techniques and processes for doing so will be presented here, and they start with how you present yourself and your ideas. We've found that many people hold back, fearing they have little if anything to give in an initial exchange. It's important to overcome this fear, and one way of doing so is to think about all the exchanges you've made throughout your life. For example, when you were a student, you exchanged your homework for a grade. In any work setting, you exchanged your work for income. Every day you exchange information, ideas, and feelings with others. Consciously or not, you have a long and continuous history of making exchanges. We're simply going to show you how to become more conscious of this exchange process and use it to initiate Networlding relationships.

Making an Exchange at Every Level of Contact

Initiating Networlding relationships becomes easier when you realize that you're not coming to the relationship empty-handed. The Networlding support exchange model was introduced in

Chapter One, where we briefly discussed the types of support net-worlders exchange with each other. Here, we'd like to go into more depth about this so that you'll be in a better position to make these exchanges when you begin to make a connection. Although exchanges can be formalized—they can involve a significant amount of time, thought, discussion, and so on—the ones that you'll use initially are more informal. You and another person will not meet for the first time and immediately begin providing each other with every possible form of support in order to pursue major opportunities. Nevertheless, unlike an initial networking contact, you do need to give something in exchange right from the beginning.

The support exchange model mirrors the hierarchical process involved in building any meaningful relationship. We've simply translated it into a tool that you can refer to in building successful exchanges. Let's look at the types of support used to initiate Net-worlding relationships effectively (Figure 6.1, a reproduction of Figure 1.1).

Emotional Support

Just because you don't know someone well or are interacting with that person in a business environment doesn't mean you should do so without any significant emotional giving. Some people feel it's "unprofessional" to reveal their feelings in business dealings or to allow a conversation to "descend" to that level. In fact, it's the best way to push the relationship beyond a superficial state.

Best-selling author Daniel Goleman's book *Working with Emotional Intelligence* refers to almost five hundred independent studies that support the importance of emotional intelligence (the ability to understand emotions and use them to promote emotional and intellectual growth in oneself and others). It is this same intelligence that exists at the foundation of all the relationships we build. It is this chemistry or lack of it that starts or stops a relationship between two people. Possessing soft skills, such as empathy, is becoming more important than possessing purely technical skills because people are increasingly relying on trust, influence, and intuition in their business dealings and less on deal making, power, and cold logic.

Figure 6.1. The Networlding Support Exchange Model.

Increasingly, people are receptive to emotional honesty and are looking for someone who not only says what he or she really feels but also is an empathic listener. An exchange of emotional support is a signal that you care about another person (and not just the project you are working on). We know young people who have initiated relationships with older influencers just by being attentive, responsive listeners. We're not referring to "fake" listening, where one pretends to care about what another person is saying. Instead, we mean expressing honest interest and concern. This expression can be as simple as sincere body language (holding eye contact, leaning closer to create spatial intimacy) or it can take the form of asking questions or relating relevant experiences in response. This is about *honoring* each relationship.

An emotional connection can be established in the opposite direction, too—for instance, when an influencer becomes more open and honest with a noninfluencer. This can be as simple as a manager taking his direct report out to lunch, telling her how her work adds value to their group and their organization, and revealing how grateful he is for her contribution. This has an especially big impact when it is done for the first time. It's sufficiently out of the ordinary that it makes an impression on the other person; it's a great initiating technique.

Giving praise unexpectedly is a good initiating technique, too. Telling people how much you appreciate what they've done when they don't expect an expression of appreciation can build a bond. When doing this isn't routine, the surprise makes the other person think: "I didn't realize that Mary understood how hard I fought for her transfer," or "Joe really gets that it was my persistence and ideas that helped the team achieve its objective." When the praise is routine—a thank-you for a raise, a show of appreciation at the successful conclusion of a project—the impact isn't as great.

Of course, we're not suggesting that you become sloppily sentimental or offer praise and listen empathically to everyone you interact with. But when you encounter someone who seems to share your values, who is an influencer, and who has goals that overlap with your own, then doing this may be a good way to initiate a relationship.

Informational Support

We live in what many call the Information Age, and indeed most people are overwhelmed by data. So the key here isn't simply to offer someone easily accessible or obvious information. A relationship should be initiated with valuable information. If you can provide someone with eye-opening facts and useful statistics, you will have changed his or her perception of you. It's as if you've become that person's private, highly effective market research firm.

Again, exchanging information support requires some preparation. You may have the world at your fingertips if you're a proficient Internet user, but you need to exercise your analytical skills to determine what another person may perceive to be important information. People who use information well in relationships are usually keen observers of the world around them. They can discern what's relevant when confronted with a huge volume of information. They're aware both of what's happening in their immediate work environment and in the outside world. They know when relevant speakers are coming to town and where interesting conferences are being held. They're aware of industry trends and different experts' interpretations of these trends.

Most of all, they are tuned in to what type of information another person needs and when. For example, Dan, who had just finished architecture school, was meeting Cindy for lunch. Cindy, the owner of a growing architectural firm, was glad to have lunch with Dan and share some career insights with him because his aunt was her good friend. Dan had been reading the newspaper before their lunch and noticed a small article buried in the back of the news section about how the mayor intended to move 25 percent of city hall staff out of their current offices and build a new structure on city-owned land. Dan had done some research about Cindy's firm in anticipation of their lunch and discovered that they had designed a number of government buildings in the past. He decided to call the mayor's office and see if an architect had been chosen for the new project. It turned out that they were in the process of taking bids. When he shared this information with Cindy, she was tremendously appreciative because neither she nor any of her people had seen the story. She was impressed that Dan had gone to the trouble to learn about her firm and call the mayor's office. What started as a lunch turned into an internship for Dan.

Knowledge Support

There's a subtle but important difference between information support and knowledge support. The former involves sharing pure data; the latter means sharing one's conclusions, educated guesses, hypotheses, and the like. In essence, the knowledge shared is based on experience. Those who receive it are impressed by someone's willingness to part with such hard-won knowledge, and it provides the leverage to move a new relationship to a higher level.

When Alvenia was first starting her career, she found a mentor—Clara—who offered great insight into how to become an executive in a nonprofit association. With Clara's guidance, Alvenia learned which organizations had the strongest, most supportive boards and which were to be avoided at all costs. When there was an opening at one of the recommended nonprofits, Alvenia was ready to respond. The knowledge Clara had shared helped Alvenia gain an introduction to one of the most active board members. From this introduction came a meeting with the board. At the meeting, Alvenia was impressive and articulate about the nuances of the board—their individual "hot buttons" and areas of conversation to avoid—in part because Clara had shared her insights. Alvenia got the position, and for many years afterward she not only continued to rely on Clara's knowledge but found herself accumulating her own storehouse of knowledge, which she freely shared with Clara to help her capitalize on opportunities.

Interestingly, Alvenia began acquiring knowledge that was useful to Clara after only six months on the job. Her perceptive observations about how her own board worked and what their needs were helped Clara land a major piece of business.

Promotional Support

Perhaps the best way to get a Networlding relationship off on the right foot is to hot-link one person to another. Hot linking also involves consciously seeking opportunities to promote your primary circle partners' strengths. By consciously keeping an eye out for connections between people, you put yourself in the position of offering invaluable promotional support. You don't have to be an influencer to provide this type of support. All it takes is being highly conscious of potential links between people and then taking action by referring or promotionally introducing one person to another. This means taking just a moment or two to share something about that person that might be of value to the other.

Promotional support has a spiral effect in the sense that it spreads quickly from one person to the next. When you inform Sue that Jane is absolutely terrific at a particular skill that she's been looking for, Sue is likely not only to call Jane but also to mention Jane's skill to someone else who needs it. This form or support is called "word-of-mouth marketing" in the business world. It is the most effective form of marketing. Networlders recognize its power and use it to grow their opportunities and those of the people whom they promote.

Promotional support is a reflex action among networlders. They are always saying things like this to people in their various circles: "You should meet Pam. She is by far the most gifted graphic designer I have seen recently. You might consider using her on your next project." Or, "You have to call Jerod. He is the best accountant I have ever worked with. Last year he saved our company thousands of dollars." Networlders have a cadre of unofficial public relations people working for them. They get the word out that John is an expert at financial consulting or that Mimi is brilliant at turnarounds. Networlders are routinely asked to interview for jobs, make presentations, and participate in other opportunities because they enjoy strong and continuous promotional support.

As you promote, so too are you promoted. This crucial exchange is one you want to establish from the very beginning of a relationship. In many ways, it's a good test of the Networlding quality of the relationship. If you promote someone to others, will he or she promote you back?

Nothing makes people more confident in you and more willing to trust you than promotional support. They know that you're taking a risk when you recommend them. You're putting your own judgment and reputation on the line. Marty, for instance, was a young product manager for a Fortune 100 company only two years out of school. He had met Charlie at a marketing association meeting and liked him immensely. Charlie was an account supervisor at an ad agency and seemed to have a grasp of corporate identity advertising. More important, Marty believed that Charlie was a "kindred spirit"; they shared similar views about their businesses as well as beliefs about appropriate (and inappropriate) career behaviors. When Marty's company fired one of its ad agencies and started a search for another one, Marty recommended to his boss's boss that they talk to Charlie. Given the volatile nature of agency-advertiser relationships and the company's ambitious advertising goals, Marty was taking a big chance. The company's marketing executives might not have liked Charlie or his agency. Or they might have hired them and then fired them for doing a poor job. Either way, Marty could suffer.

But Marty had the courage of his convictions, made the recommendation, and everything worked out. In fact, Charlie eventually recommended Marty for a top marketing position with another of his agency's Fortune 100 clients.

Promotional support initiates relationships in all sorts of ways. It not only helps you establish a relationship with the individual you're supporting but also gets your name out there in the exchange. You'll find that people call you and ask you to attend meetings that you never dreamed of hearing about at this stage in your career.

Other Support Exchanges, and Fulfillment

We leave the description of the remaining forms of exchange to the next chapters, because they are best understood in the context of the next Networlding steps. This is because until you have gone through the process of Networlding several times it is unlikely that you will exchange wisdom, transformational opportunities, or community upon meeting with someone. (In Chapter Ten we offer you insights into what this would look like, if you wish to take a sneak preview.)

Still, the experience of fulfillment—the emotion that surrounds the Networlding support exchange model—can be realized at any time. This is because when you take the time to become aware of another, looking for those connections that really matter, you will experience fulfillment. Your conversations will be more meaningful. You will discover that certain people are better partners than others, and you will wisely choose to spend time only with those who really understand what exchanging is all about.

Ingredients of Effective Exchanges

It's not only *what* is exchanged that counts in Networlding but also *how* it is exchanged. As much informational or emotional support as you might give and receive when you meet someone, the relationship requires a firmer bond to grow on. If the other person doesn't feel she has anything in common with you or is suspicious of your motives, you will have difficulty initiating a Networlding relationship.

Starting an effective exchange is all about building trust. You need to trust each other sufficiently to exchange the valuable ideas, information, and other forms of support that launch the relationship.

As you build trust, it accumulates into *opportunity capital*. This capital gives both people the confidence in each other that is necessary to explore opportunities together or to make each other aware of an opportunity.

You do many practical things to initiate a relationship—make phone calls, set up meetings, have lunch, exchange support—but while undertaking all these actions you must also develop trust. Let's look at some of the ways in which this can be done.

Trust develops over time and is in part a function of free-flowing exchanges. The trust continuum shown in Figure 6.2 illustrates this principle.

Trust adds depth and breadth to Networlding relationships. It helps people move past the rough spots of failed opportunities or disagreements, providing a connection that is more powerful than trying to do a deal together. In many ways, trust makes people want to work together; it provides a comfort level as well as an environment in which partners can be open and honest with each other.

Trust isn't earned instantly, but you can start building it from the moment you meet a potential Networlding partner. Here are the steps to take.

Points of Commonality

Points of commonality are pieces of information you have in common with others. You identify the common connections by asking questions that identify your new contact's background. For exam-

Figure 6.2. The Trust Continuum.

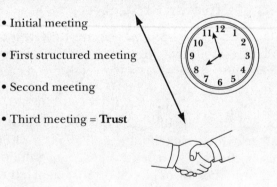

- Initial meeting

- First structured meeting

- Second meeting

- Third meeting = **Trust**

ple, you might ask, "George, what company are you with?" or "What brings you to this association?" Notice that these questions are open-ended. They require more than a yes or no answer. Open-ended questions encourage others to open up. You want to encourage your new contacts to share as much information about themselves as possible. Each nugget of information will help you identify common interests that will lead to a rapport being developed. The more common interests you share, the more potential there is for trust. Essentially, you're establishing a comfort level that is a precursor to trust.

If your contact says, "I'm in the telecommunications industry," probe further to assess the connections in your area of interest. If you're in banking, you might respond, "That's very interesting. Do you currently work with anyone in my field?" Chances are, your new connection—depending on the number of years he has been in the industry—will have relationships with others in your field. It is wise, however, to postpone asking who else they know. Asking too much too soon creates suspicion rather than trust; it stamps you as a networker of the worst sort. If this person offers information without too much probing then it's likely he'll be similarly generous with referrals. Save this conversation for a second or third meeting, when you've reached a stage where you both feel more comfortable about this type of exchange.

Your interests and skills are other areas where you may have something in common. Ideally, an individual's interests and skills flow from his or her values, such as an interest in volunteer work (people who value generosity) or a skill at writing (people who value artistic expression). An interest or skill may be dormant—something you loved in the past but haven't had time for recently, like playing the violin or coaching kids' sports teams. Reflect on your interests and skills. Then list them in any order as you brainstorm, writing down the first ideas that come to your mind. The list you develop will provide you with areas to explore with new contacts where you might have something in common.

Example: Top Points of Commonality   Your Turn

Walking
Dancing

Playing golf
Writing
Seeing movies
Doing volunteer work
Traveling
Spending time with family
Listening to (or playing) music
Being spiritually active

Now prioritize your list. Think for a couple of minutes before you begin to identify which interests are most significant to you at this time in your life. Your choices may surprise you. You may have an interest that you thought wasn't important, but when compared with your other interests really is. Once again, the point is to be intentional about initiating relationships. If you do not think about and reflect on your interests and skills, you may go into a meeting unaware of points of commonality. Or you might make false assumptions about what really interests you, leading you to share false points of commonality. Therefore, take a few minutes to prioritize what really matters to you.

| *Example: Top Points of* | *Your Turn* |
| *Commonality, Revised* | |

Being spiritually active
Spending time with family
Writing
Doing volunteer work
Listening to (or playing) music
Seeing movies
Traveling
Walking
Dancing
Playing golf

Keep these interests and skills in mind, especially the ones at the top of your list. When you initiate a relationship, find a way to communicate these interests. It may be as simple as noticing a bowling trophy on a desk and using it as a segue to talk about your bowling league. Or you may notice books on spirituality behind someone's desk and relate your own experiences as a yoga instructor. Sometimes it's not so easy, and you have to ask a few questions that revolve around your interests. This may feel a bit awkward at first, but you'll find that if you really care about an interest, you are naturally curious about whether others share that interest. When two people find they have something in common it immediately deepens the relationship. It doesn't create deep and abiding trust, but it nudges the relationship in that direction. As you'll see, the next step moves you further down this road.

Points of Credibility

This isn't about bragging. It's not about name dropping. It is about modestly and honestly communicating your accomplishments, strengths, and unique experiences. What you want to get across is that you've done something significant or something different that you're proud of. At the very least, you're demonstrating that you're a person who has done things or is capable of doing things. You're suggesting that you've worked hard, become proficient, and achieved something because of your proficiency. People tend to trust people who have achieved something unique or important in their lives more than those who seem (usually because they haven't communicated it) to have accomplished nothing.

Sandy had just started her own business in marketing. She invested hours attending networking events trying to acquire new clients. Until she began to reflect introspectively, however, she was unaware of her distinguishing points of credibility, which positioned her uniquely to others. Sandy would introduce herself and her company by saying, "I'm Sandy and I'm new to the area. I just started my own marketing company. If you know of anyone who needs marketing services, please let me know. Here is my card."

But Sandy never mentioned that although she was a neophyte entrepreneur, she had five years of experience in marketing at a top marketing consultancy. She also failed to mention that she had spent the last three years working on marketing business-to-business strategies for companies such as Amazon.com. When she revised her introductory remarks to include these points of credibility, Sandy found that people responded to her differently. Before, she felt a "blank wall" when she tried to initiate a conversation. After, she saw a light go on in at least some people's eyes—people who realized she had something to offer. The possibility of a mutually beneficial relationship existed, and they trusted what Sandy said more than when she had failed to make herself credible.

Here is an exercise that will help you uncover your hidden points of credibility. Write down your points of credibility. Then, ask your friends and relatives to identify what they believe these points are.

Example: Top Points of Credibility	*Your Turn*

MBA degree
Strength in speaking
Good knowledge of computers

| *Example: Top Points of Credibility* | *Your Turn* |
| *Recognized by Family, Friends,* | |
Colleagues	

Caring, involved parent
Enthusiastic nature
Loyal friend

Like thousands of others who have done this exercise, you will undoubtedly find that there are a number of unidentified points. Jane, for instance, was surprised to learn that her family and coworkers thought that patience was her virtue. She had never conceived of her ability to be patient as an attribute, but after receiving this feedback became much more conscious of how it served others; she was a great listener and didn't become frustrated when things didn't go according to plan. When she went to a job interview, Jane made it a point to mention that her mother told her she had "the patience of a saint." The interviewer, Lina, didn't have a job that fit Jane's skills. But she was working for a fast-growth, high-tech company with numerous young people, many of whom lacked patience (and alienated older managers because of this trait). When there was an opening in the company that fit Jane's skills, Lina immediately called her for a round of interviews. Jane was offered and accepted the position, due in no small part to Lina's enthusiastic recommendation.

Points of commonality and credibility are tools that anyone can use to build a rapport that leads to trust. By using these tools when you initiate a relationship, you increase the odds of Networlding. In addition, commonality and credibility jump-start a process that might take a long time to unfold. At one event we held, there were approximately 150 attendees. Participants were seated at tables of eight and asked to explore their points of credibility and commonality. A young woman who had just graduated with a degree in physical therapy—with a focus on cycling injuries—sat at one of the tables. Serendipitously seated next to her was a young man who was an Olympic cyclist! If the woman had not been willing to share her particular skill with the cyclist, they would have never developed into Networlding partners. Shyness, preoccupation with other matters, and the tendency to jump to conclusions based on appearance are all factors that make us reluctant to search for common ground.

Networkers spend most of their time searching for new relationships and discarding those they view as old and worn out. In fact, there may be great potential in those old relationships, but they do not bother to explore it. Sharing points of commonality and credibility not only is a good way to initiate a relationship but can revive ones that seemed moribund.

Matched Values

The third building block to a trusting relationship involves values. Previously, we talked about how you need to identify your values and build your goals and plans around them. With those values in mind, you now must learn how to identify the values of others relatively quickly in order to determine if they are compatible with your own.

Begin by recalling your top value, which you located in Step One, Chapter Three. Keep it in mind as you initiate a relationship so that you can determine if the other individual possesses values that are the same or similar. People sometimes think it takes a long time to discover another person's values. Although it's true that some people reveal very little about their inner selves, especially in business settings, you'll find that you can elicit information about another person's values relatively easily if you do the following:

Communicate Values

Talk about what's most meaningful in your life and work. Whether you value the environment, innovation, or honesty, make it known to the other person. Explain why this is important to you. In most instances, the other person will respond in kind. It may be that he'll disagree with what you value and talk about his oppositional values, but that's fine. You've discovered an incompatibility that will prevent a Networlding relationship from forming.

Find Meaning Beneath the Words

People may not feel comfortable saying, "My value is thus and such." Or they may be unwilling to spell out their values in an initial meeting. Therefore, listen to how they speak and watch their body language. When do their voices become intense and their words eloquent; when do they sound as if they're digging in and unwilling to waver? You can "feel" when someone is really passionate about an issue—and beneath that passion is a value.

Offer What-If Scenarios

Hypothetical scenarios often free up people to answer honestly and according to their values. In real-life situations, they may worry about expressing their true feelings because they think they'll offend or say something that will come back to haunt them. Therefore, ask what-ifs. For instance: "What if you knew a supplier you were using was lying to you about costs. Even if he had worked with your company for years and provided good service, would you allow the relationship to continue?" If so, honesty is not this person's top value.

Shared values often lead to opportunity-producing relationships. Claire met Harold on a plane while traveling to a sales call in Boston. She learned that Harold had a real passion for addressing workplace violence. Claire, who had graduated with a degree in social work but was now in sales, was intrigued by how dedicated Harold was to this cause and how much he believed in antiviolence principles. They discussed his involvement with an initiative to stop workplace violence in his organization and decided to collaborate by getting Claire's company involved. Today, the two organizations host an electronic anger forum. At the forum, they involve other organizations to share best practices for ending violence in the workplace and in the families of employees.

The Right Tone and Timing

The "antinetworlder" is someone who sounds glib, slick, and superficial. He may say all the right things, but the way he says them and when he says them turns you off. When you initiate relationships and attempt to build trust, you need to establish the right tone and timing so that your words match the situations.

Sincerity is crucial. As painful or difficult as it might be, you must say what you believe. This can be difficult if you know what you're saying will turn off an influencer you're meeting for the first time. No doubt, you're tempted to say what you think that person wants to hear. But networlders are adept at spotting insincerity. You may think you sound convincing, but people often can spot a disingenuous tone. Besides, sooner or later the other individual will discover your insincerity, and that will end the relationship after you've put in a great deal of relationship work. Therefore, say what you believe and your tone will reflect this sincerity.

Timing isn't difficult if you're "other-focused." Through their eyes and body language as well as their words, you can sense when it's appropriate to say something. If you watch and listen closely, you can see a disapproving glance when you start to talk business during a social event. If you pay attention, you can determine if someone is open to a discussion about beliefs and values. People don't always provide open invitations to discuss the subjects we've outlined here. If they're smiling and their eyes are warm and friendly, then your timing is right. If you notice a frown or a tensing of neck and shoulder muscles, then back off and wait for a more opportune time.

Matched Communication Styles

This is a simple but effective technique to make another person feel as if you're speaking the same language. Most people demonstrate a predisposition for one of three communication styles: visual, auditory, or kinesthetic (feeling). Identify the other's preferred style. If you are faced with a person who uses phrases like "I see" often, mirror his vocabulary by saying things like, "I see your point." With people who are auditory, you might say, "I hear what you're saying." With those who have a more kinesthetic vocabulary, you might say, "I understand how you feel." Expressing yourself in each of these ways requires a little practice. At first, you may feel awkward as you attempt to respond in kind to the other person's style. Obviously, you don't want to keep repeating "I understand how you feel" ad infinitum; you must develop your own way of mirroring a feeling style. In any case, people usually don't consciously recognize that you are adapting to their vocabulary; instead, this approach triggers a connection with their subconscious. They sense a connection with you because of how you're responding, and this helps build trust quickly.

A Few Points of Etiquette

In a nutshell, networlders initiate relationships in polite, courteous, empathic ways. Rightly or wrongly, people make judgments about others based on social manners and mannerisms. Discourteous behavior, even if you didn't intend to be discourteous, can create distrust and make another person unwilling to exchange a single fact with you (let alone emotional support). The following rules of etiquette will help you avoid Networlding faux pas:

- *Follow up.* Advise the people you meet that you will follow up, then deliver in a timely fashion.
- *Maintain eye contact.* Nothing communicates insincerity more than letting your eyes roam around the room (in search of a better contact). If you want to convey a lack of credibility, stare at your shoes while you talk. However, if you want to show others you truly care about them and what they are saying, maintain eye contact. Just avoid staring.
- *Smile.* Smiling shows people that you are open and eager to listen to them. More than anything you say or do, a genuine smile is one of the most powerful Networlding tools. Most of us think we smile much more than we actually do.
- *Locate people who are standing alone.* You know how you feel when you are alone. Helping someone else feel welcome by acting as a host, even if you are a guest, will also help you feel more at ease. It will communicate to anyone who is watching that you are considerate and compassionate.

- *Give first, before you ask for anything.* In every conversation, look first to make others comfortable and only second to address your own needs.
- *Avoid social butterflyitis.* Spend a reasonable amount of time with each contact. Don't flit from person to person in a desperate attempt to connect. Be gracious when you excuse yourself after a conversation has ended.
- *Be expressive.* Be an expressive listener with your body and your face. Demonstrate that you're actively listening even when you aren't saying anything.

Nine Strategies for Establishing Meaningful Contact

Developing trust and exchanging various forms of support are the two challenges for aspiring networlders when they initiate relationships. In most instances, people aren't accustomed to approaching people in this manner. These are the big hurdles that must be cleared in order to begin Networlding effectively.

But there are also a number of smaller hurdles, most related to being proactive in relationship building. Whether you're networking or Networlding, it's difficult to approach people. The following tips are designed to ease your initiating path and establish the types of Networlding connections you're seeking.

Start by Seeking Relationships in the "Easiest" Places

Look at all the possible opportunities that are in front of you—such as these, for example: you are required by your company to develop new referral sources or prospects over the course of the next year, you are asked to be a spokesperson on behalf of your company, you are asked to take an active role in sharing knowledge between departments, you are asked to build strategic alliances with outside vendors, or you are encouraged to contribute to your community through volunteerism.

You can piggyback your Networlding efforts onto these common activities. Because they all require you to initiate relationships, you can use them to practice your approach. For example, let's say your organization wants you to attend a three-day industry conference. You dread the event because you're going alone and furthermore you're worried about being away from your office at this time of year. If you allow all your worries and fears to dominate your thinking, you'll mope through the conference and meet few if any people. But let's say you take a Networlding approach. The first thing you do is find out from your top customers their concerns about growing their businesses. When you mention that you will be attending the conference, you discover that one or two of their employees are also going. You make a plan to attend a couple of sessions with them to address some of their issues, and they appreciate your willingness to make this effort.

But your efforts don't end there. After viewing the conference flyer, you identify the industry influencers who are giving presentations. A couple of the presenters have written books, and you visit Web sites such as Amazon.com to locate information on their books as well as on the presenters themselves. Once you've gathered this information, you e-mail these presenters with questions from your top customers, demonstrating a knowledge of who the presenters are and the issues that concern them. It is likely at this point that two or three of the presenters will respond with answers to your customers' questions, so before the conference begins you get in touch with your customers and share these responses. It's also likely that at least one of the presenters, appreciative of your knowledge and intelligent inquiry, will send you a copy of his book and suggest that you get together at the conference to talk. You arrange a date to do so. But before the conference you do your homework, gathering information that you think would be of interest to the presenter as well as ideas and opportunities that you suspect might interest him. Of course, you have no guarantee that this relationship will pan out and become a Networlding one, but you have prepared yourself for the type of mutual exchange that will make it much more likely to happen.

We're not suggesting that you must follow this exact scenario or that every presenter at every conference will respond positively (though people with Networlding mind-sets probably will). Our point is that initiating relationships requires a proactive, optimistic attitude. You may start out trying to establish a Networlding relationship with a customer and end up building one with a keynote speaker (or both). The key is to believe that *anything is possible* when you start exploring new relationships. Repeat this as your mantra before you go to sleep each night. Visualize all the possible relationships you might foster if you just look at your routine activities and attempt to make more of them than you ordinarily do.

Be Prepared

What happens when you go to an event where you know no one? How can you possibly initiate an exchange if there is no common ground? When you feel like the new kid in school, it's often difficult to say or do anything that will call attention to yourself.

It's important to acknowledge that you have these feelings. Imagine yourself walking into a room of strangers. You know no one and three hours stretch in front of you devoid of warm and friendly colleagues with whom you can talk freely. Instead, you see people who appear to have no intention of including you in their conversations. As much as you want to initiate a conversation or rehearse an opening line about an industry issue, your mouth is dry and your heart is pounding when you just think about approaching someone. Before you know it, you leave the event prematurely without having talked to a single soul.

If you want to avoid this scenario, you can't go in cold. Networlders are sticklers for preparation, especially when they will be in situations where they will encounter a sea of unfamiliar faces. One preparatory tactic involves contacting the head of the membership committee or the person in charge of an event you want to attend. These people are in the business of making sure you benefit from the event; their job is to make sure you find it worthwhile. This gives you a certain amount of influence in their arena. Use this influence to initiate relationships with these people.

For instance, contact the coordinator of an event and say something along these lines: "I'm planning on attending your upcoming event and I'd like to know more about your organization." This open-ended request will often lead to a friendly conversation about the organization and how it can benefit attendees. Push the conversation further by noting that the organization sounds as if it's doing valuable things for its members and asking if there's someone you might talk to about lending your efforts to help it meet its goals. What you're attempting to do here is suggest that you want to know how you can be of value to the organization. Many event coordinators and program chairpeople are very receptive to this type of inquiry because they've usually given so much to the organization and are often desperate for help.

Thus, this approach invites reciprocity. Many times, these people will accept your offer of assistance and be very receptive to your requests for help. For instance, they might introduce you to an attendee who sends many employees to the seminars. This person is likely to be an influencer who might make a good Networlding partner. Or they might introduce you to someone at the event itself because you've taken the time and made the effort to establish a relationship with them. Instead of going into the event cold, you've created a relationship with the one person who knows the most about most of the people at the event. You've exchanged a bit of time and effort on behalf of the organization for a pathway to other members of the organization. This is a great start, but before you go further, you need to have a good understanding of the different types of exchanges at your disposal to initiate relationships.

Seek Connections Even If You Don't Want To

Even veteran networlders get apprehensive at times, especially when they're in unfamiliar places and uncomfortable situations. There are times when they would rather do anything other than meet another person. But they seek connections continuously, overcoming short-term anxiety with a vision of long-term opportunities in mind.

Recognize that fear is normal in any new social interaction but don't become overwhelmed by it. Keep the fear at bay by envisioning the incredible networld you're going to construct if you keep making connections. Think about lying on a hot beach on a summer day and wanting to plunge into the water. You stick a toe in and it feels cold. You may be tempted to retreat to your blanket to swelter. But if you're smart, you recognize that you'll become used to the water and that it will eventually feel great. Plunge into relationships the same way, but be sure to keep your eyes open and breathe regularly.

Learn from Rejection

Overwhelmingly, people fear rejection. As Jack Lemmon once said, it is not the rejection itself but the actual fear of it that will kill you. When we reach outside of ourselves for approval, we are guaranteed to find a certain amount of rejection. This is very natural. Sometimes you are rejected because other people don't understand you; at other times it is for silly reasons—you look like someone's former spouse.

You need to look at rejection objectively. If you're being rejected for silly reasons—the other person is a jerk, he doesn't like your tie—then acknowledge that the rejection is meaningless and move on. However, you may be rejected for valid reasons by a prospective networlder. Perhaps you have demonstrated an unwillingness to exchange support, or your manner or words makes the other person suspicious. If you believe there's a valid reason behind the rejection, explore it. Ask other people who may have witnessed the encounter what they thought you did wrong. Ask the person in question! Don't do it in a confrontational manner but rather as a true learner: "I'm sorry you declined my invitation to meet after the conference, but I'm just curious: Did I say something offensive or am I missing something?"

We've found that people deal with rejection well when they keep an antirejection statement in mind. This is a brief statement that reveals who you are honestly and positively. For instance: "I am a kind, honest person who sincerely wants to succeed and help others whenever possible." When you own who you are, you won't be at the mercy of who others imply you are by their rejection. Repeating that statement to yourself will help you take the emotion out of a rejection and give you the opportunity to analyze it logically and see if there is anything to learn from it.

Create a Positive Image

Some people aren't even aware of the image they project. Others work hard to define and project a very specific persona. Networlders, obviously, do the latter. Expert image consultant Susan Fignar of Image Works Wonders (www.imageworks.com) in Chicago says that we all have an image we project in the first thirty seconds of meeting someone. This image can lead the way toward deeper interactions.

What image do you want to project? What image do you actually project? Answer the first question, and then inquire of friends and business associates about the latter. If there's a gap or contradiction, you need to work on your appearance, attitude, and behaviors, all of which combine to craft an image. Again, the key is to be conscious of who you are and how you're coming across. Networlders are self-aware without being self-obsessed. They think about how their words and actions affect others. Just being conscious of your own words and actions will help you create a positive image.

Build Appreciation into Your Conversations with Others

As we said earlier, showing appreciation is important. Look for things to appreciate in others. For example, if someone is a good listener or good communicator, comment on it. When people are complimented, they feel better about themselves and thus are more open to sharing. You shouldn't be dishonest or deliver compliments in an ingratiating manner. But if you really appreciate something about someone, convey it sincerely and forcefully.

Also communicate your appreciation for the way in which they say something. In other words, if someone suddenly is very animated about a point or you hear the excitement in his voice, this is an opportunity to be appreciative. If someone says to you, "I just started a new business and I've been working seven days a week for three months," try saying something like this, "That must be stressful; you must really care about your business to work that hard."

Ask the Same Question Twice

To encourage others to answer questions with forethought rather than superficially, try the tactic of asking the same question twice. For example, ask, "Why did you decide to join this association?" Later, you might ask, "What was that reason again for joining this association?" People will take your question as a sign of interest, not as a sign of senility. By really listening and asking again sincerely, you're communicating a genuine interest in the person behind the position. One networlder found that when he asked, "How are you?" he would receive one response. But then when he asked again, "How are you really?" the respondent would open up and share much more freely. An exchange would take place.

Ask for an Introduction

Don't be afraid to ask for an introduction from someone you've just met if you feel a real connection has been made. There is a fine line here. You don't want to overstep the bounds and ask for something when you haven't had a chance to give anything in return. At the same time, some initial conversations create immediate knowledge and even emotional support exchanges, especially when Networlding tactics are used. If you sense a connection, if you believe you share values and goals with another person, don't be reluctant to ask for a bit of help. If a good relationship has been established, people will be happy to introduce you to someone they know because they feel good about you. Note that asking for introductions is different from referral. Referrals should be requested once someone knows enough about you to make a conscious referral, which is a recommendation of observed skills.

Arrange Another Conversation

We're all busy, but unless you take the time to grow a relationship, you will discover how quickly the initial rapport is lost. It's amazing how many people fail to follow up on a great connection. Sometimes they assume that the other person will call them; sometimes they have every intention of making a follow-up call after a few days but become distracted, too much time passes, and the relationship loses its momentum. Therefore, don't leave a great initiating meeting without suggesting getting together or talking at a specific future date.

Experiencing Transformational Opportunities

You're not initiating Networlding relationships just for the sake of it. Even at this early stage of the process, it's possible to meet incredible people and make incredible plans. The holy grail of Networlding is *transformational opportunities*. As the term implies, these are opportunities that can transform your career, your business, even your life. They occur as a natural outgrowth when two people subscribe to the core Networlding belief that anything is possible. These opportunities are transformational because they speak to your heart rather than to your head. In other words, your networld partners have listened to what matters most to you, what stirs your passion, and have acted as a conduit to opportunities beyond what you think are currently possible.

What we hope we are leaving you with as we conclude this chapter is the understanding that initiating a relationship can quickly lead to an exchange that goes beyond ideas, facts, and emotional support. It can also lead to transformational opportunities. This only occurs, however, when you grow and nurture your relationships. If you're following this Networlding methodology, it's entirely possible that you'll soon be exchanging opportunities with your partner that will yield dramatic and positive changes in your personal and professional life. With Networlding, transformational opportunities happen regularly, by choice, rather than sporadically, by chance.

CHAPTER SEVEN

Step Five: Grow and Nurture Relationships

Once you have initiated an exchange and found someone who has the potential to become your Networlding partner, the next step is to grow and nurture that relationship to achieve vibrant, collaborative exchanges. Networlding relationships are dynamic, unlike the static relationships that are typical of networking, and this chapter is designed to provide you with the techniques to grow and nurture the relationships you establish.

This is a challenging assignment for most of us because we feel that we lack the time required to develop relationships. Ironically, despite the interconnectedness of the modern technological world, we are more disconnected from others than ever before. Given the time constraints we all operate under, it's crucial to initiate the right relationships with the right people. If you can follow the steps of the previous chapters, you won't have to waste your time in a frantic search for contacts. You can focus on growing and nurturing relationships with people who possess true Networlding potential.

This process provides personal fulfillment and transformational opportunities. Although this fulfillment and these opportunities can occur in the initiating stage, they're more common after relationships have matured. Once Networlding relationships deepen, their effect is felt in many ways by many people. As Emerson once said, "It is one of the most beautiful compensations of this life that no man can sincerely try to help another without helping himself." Nurturing relationships means helping others through an ongoing series of exchanges, and there's great satisfaction in using your skill,

127

knowledge, and empathy to help others capitalize on opportunities. This "good work" is its own reward, but it also pays dividends to the giver. You'll discover that you can make a difference for the many and for yourself.

Maximizing Networlding Interactions: General Guidelines

Nurturing a relationship requires a conscious time commitment so that exchanges can take place. The first thing to do after a relationship has been initiated, therefore, is to schedule time for regular interactions. We've found that even ten-minute monthly conversations can yield great opportunities. Set aside time for sharing opportunities with your networld partners at least once a month. It is great if you can meet in person, but scheduled phone conversations can also work as long as you make sure you have a conversation around one of the types of exchanges described in the support exchange model. For example, you might spend the first five minutes updating one another on all the new people you've met, conferences you've learned of, Web sites you've discovered, and so on. Any of these new connections can be opportunities for one another. At the very least, connect by e-mail monthly.

Because you may not have much time available for these monthly interactions, you want to maximize your time together. A relationship won't be nurtured just because you meet or talk regularly. You need to deal with issues of substance. To make the most of each interaction, here are some tips.

Develop a List of the Top Three Things You Want to Accomplish When You Talk

Too often, people become distracted by secondary issues or are sidetracked by unimportant subjects. The need is to be intentional. By saying to yourself, "First, talk about our careers or business in general. Second, exchange information about projects we are pursuing or working on. Third, talk about new people we have met who we might refer one another to," you increase the odds of accomplishing what's important. This organized approach will not only help you feel good about the relationship but also make your partner appreciative of your focus.

Share a Little About Your Background

Relationships won't grow if both people don't have some sense of the other's history. You don't have to tell the other person your life story, but you should reveal at least some salient details from your work life and how your career or business has evolved. If you have a Web site or home page, or perhaps articles you've written or ones written about you on the Internet, referring your networld partners to these sources really shortens the time it takes to build strong rapport.

Set Up Expectations with Your Partners from the Start

You might say, for example, "I want to focus on just one opportunity over the next six months, and I'm putting together a team and strategy related to it. Do you have any ideas?" Be sure to allow your partner to express his or her expectations for the interaction. Although the expectations might dovetail—you may both be interested in working on your opportunity—it's also possible that he or she has different expectations (and opportunities) that you need to address. If you communicate expectations you will avoid one-sided or unsatisfying interactions that prevent relationships from growing.

Brainstorm

Just as many authors create (these are kinesthetic communicators) when they brainstorm, you need to brainstorm in your exchanges. The Networlding exchange summary (Exhibit 7.1) provides the foundation for brainstorming during an exchange. Intellectual activity is the glue for Networlding relationships and builds mutual respect, helping the relationship evolve. You can fill out the summary during the exchange or use it merely as a reference tool to make sure you cover all possible opportunities.

Withhold Judgment

The goal is to build rapport and not to tear down the other person's ideas. Certainly you should be able to debate and disagree with your new partner, but you should not suggest that his ideas

Exhibit 7.1. Networlding Exchange Summary.

Networlding Partner	Meeting Information
Name	today's date/time:
Title	last meeting date/time:
Company Name	next meeting date/time:
Address	
City/State/Zip	
Telephone	

Section I—Referral Log of Names			
Name	Telephone	Address	For What?

Section II—Project Collaborations

Section III—To Do (Prioritize)
1)
2)
3)
4)
5)

Section IV—(A) "Who Do You Know" or (B) "Do You Know"

are ill conceived. What you need to do is give the other person the benefit of the doubt and concentrate on communicating non-judgmentally. If others feel that you're judging them before you really "know" them or understand what their ideas are about, they'll be less open to you and the relationship won't grow.

Ask "Who Do You Know?" and "Do You Know X?"

Introducing and being introduced to other people through Net-worlding leads to gratitude and respect, which help relationships blossom. Therefore, you want to mine all possible relationships in your interactions. "Who do you know?" is an open-ended question that invites people to search their mental database in creative ways. "Do you know X?" is a more targeted question designed to establish a connection with a specific individual. Asking both increases the odds that you'll cover all the people bases.

Stay Focused on the Networlding Exchange Summary

The Networlding Exchange Summary is also a useful tool to keep you focused and productive. It will also help you and your Net-worlding partners experience a truly reciprocal relationship. Always start off with emotional, informational, knowledge, and pro-motional support before talking about leads and referrals that evolve when you talk about transformational opportunities. You will develop a rapport if you establish a foundation of mutual sup-port and exchange first, and then move on to "people" and oppor-tunity exchanges.

Determine How Someone Might Fit with Others in Your Circles

You don't have to wait for the other person to ask for an introduc-tion. Be proactive and consider how your partner and someone else in your circle might mesh. For example, a transformational oppor-tunity arose for Thomas, a consultant, because Marnie recognized that his creative personality was perfect for a project her friend Jane was leading at a major corporation. Jane had told her how much she wished she could find a truly innovative consultant to help her with the project, and Marnie suspected that Thomas and Jane would click.

Maximizing Networlding Interactions: Specific Steps

Relationships, including Networlding relationships, often grow and develop haphazardly. But sometimes relationships can grow in a straighter, more consistent direction if you use certain strategies. The following may help.

Organize Your Thoughts and Actions

Be prepared not only for initiating a relationship but also for nurturing it. This means determining what you're going to discuss in advance and putting it in writing. You don't want to come to a Networlding meeting empty-handed. List your ideas, questions, and the information you want to share. During the meeting itself, review these notes and make a verbal or written agreement about what you're going to do as a result of what you've shared with others. Creating action items and plans for following through lifts the conversation to a higher level. This will not only make you both feel as if you've accomplished something but also will increase the chance that you *do* follow through. Things don't slip through the cracks when you're organized. By being prepared and organized before the meeting, you demonstrate that you care enough about the other person to take this step, enhancing the quality of the relationship.

Keep Your Discussions Current

Don't dwell on people you knew in the past or information that is old news. The fresher the information, the better it is to grow the relationship. If you refer your Networlding partner to someone who no longer does what you thought he did or pass on information that is out of date, you have given a worthless gift. Topical, timely exchanges fuel relationship growth.

Exchange with your Networlding partner any current information you have gathered. Offer the latest news, introduce people with whom you've recently come in contact, and alert them to events (workshops, seminars, and so on) that you've just attended or plan to attend. New information and new contacts or opportunities with current productive Networlding partners will generate the greatest number of new opportunities for both parties in the shortest time because you're less likely to be following old trails that lead nowhere. This is because you and your partners will have your energy focused on developing energizing opportunities that may benefit many. For example, say you hear from a partner that she has just met someone who is building an Internet company. Start a discussion about the needs of the company and explore all the people in your networld who can be helpful.

Overlap Your Circles

Become highly conscious about who is in your primary, secondary, and tertiary circles and share the names of these people with your partner (and vice versa). Each of you needs to open these circles to the other. This can be a challenging process, not only because people are sometimes reluctant to be open about their connections but also because it requires time and effort to delineate every member of each circle.

In the previous chapters, we suggested a method for creating your circles. You and your partner can use this method here to identify various people who might be of help. It's an act of great generosity to open these circles to others, and a sign of great trust.

It's also important to identify the level of influence that all the people have with the others in their circle. In the Networlding exchange summary, use the section called "rank" to discuss the degree of influence your Networlding partner currently has with a particular connection. The scale runs from 1 to 5, with 1 connoting a low degree of influence and 5 suggesting a very high degree of influence. The ranking is useful as a tool to prioritize who you will each contact first and what the likelihood is of developing a stronger relationship with that individual.

We've found that it's useful to bring business cards of the people in your circles to meetings with Networlding partners. One networlder brought along a stack of business cards tied up with a red rubber band to use as a conversation tool during every exchange. She was constantly surprised by the number of people with whom her networld partners had connections—old school friends, colleagues they had lost touch with, even family members who both knew. The business cards triggered dozens of rich connections and introductions. It was also very easy to make connections because each card had a phone number and e-mail address. Another option is to bring your Palm Pilots and swap database contacts. Both strategies are useful in optimizing your exchanges.

Create Action Steps

All talk and no action leads you around in circles rather than toward a goal. Therefore, as we suggested earlier, be sure not to leave an interaction without talking about what each of you will do between now and the next time you meet. Discuss what you can do between this meeting and the next to provide each other with emotional, informational, knowledge, and promotional support. For instance, if you are planning to attend a particular event or meeting, ask if there's someone you can talk to for your partner or information you can obtain. Ask your Networlding partner how you should position her at a conference you're attending; how should you describe her particular brand of expertise. The Networlding exchange summary encourages an equal exchange. Therefore, use it as often as possible.

As a result of this step, Networlding partners Debbie and Eric created an opportunity together to market their respective services to a professional organization of association executives. They realized this opportunity when Eric asked what he could do to support Debbie. She mentioned she would like to begin speaking to professional organizations, and Eric gave her the lead to the organization's programming chairperson, whom he had met socially a few months ago. Debbie had no trouble making arrangements to present to the group. As a mutual exchange she mentioned Eric, a marketing consultant, as a good resource. In fact, she made a special effort to devote a few minutes of her presentation to Eric's area of expertise.

Neither Debbie nor Eric would have benefited from these opportunities if they hadn't made a conscious effort to turn talk into action. They asked the right questions of each other and made a concerted effort to do things that would help each other.

Summarize What You Have Exchanged and Set the Next Meeting Date

This helps each Networlding partner fulfill his or her commitments. However, you shouldn't do this as a form of one-upmanship or complaint ("I gave you three leads and you only gave me two").

Rather than quantifying the exchange, concentrate on the quality of the positive giving that occurred. Do it in the form of a thank-you: "I really appreciate that idea you shared with me." When you summarize the giving, it creates a good, nurturing feeling.

Setting the next meeting date might seem obvious but it's a step that can easily be overlooked. Again, you need to be intentional about this action. If you're not, too much time will pass and it will become awkward to contact the other person. By setting the date at the end of the interaction, you communicate that you enjoyed this meeting and are looking forward to getting together again. True networlders really do look forward to the next meeting. They are kindred spirits who create fulfillment through connection. The exchanges that take place are at the very least stimulating and at the very most transformational.

Learning How to Communicate on a More Meaningful Level

Networlding exchanges depend on regular and meaningful communication. You will never nurture and grow a relationship unless you make an effort to schedule in-person meetings and supplement them with phone conversations. Communication is the gateway to the exchanges we discussed in the previous chapter. Only when you become comfortable and practiced at communicating with each other will you exchange emotional, informational, knowledge, and promotional support.

What we're addressing here is the frequency and quality of communication. The former is a concept that's relatively easy to grasp; you simply need to make an effort to talk at least once a month. The quality issue, however, is a bit more tricky. Most of us think we're communicating on deep, meaningful levels when we're really just skirting the surface. Take a look at the following communication questions and see if you can answer them affirmatively.

Are You Aware of Your Partner's Communication Style?

In the previous chapter, we talked about communication styles in terms of auditory, visual, and kinesthetic. But you don't need those "fancy" terms to figure out your partner's style. Some people are talkers who enjoy pontificating; others are listeners who love to hear others speak. There are individuals who get to the point quickly and can't stand it when others don't do the same. Others like to engage in a sort of communication dance where partners waltz around before they get to the point. Ideally, your partner is also aware of your style and you both can adapt accordingly— which brings us to our next question.

Are You Able to Speak the Same Language?

Part of nurturing a relationship involves being tuned in to the way another person expresses himself and adopting that language. This "mirroring" helps facilitate consensus and understanding, demonstrating a sensitivity not only to what is said but also to how it is said; it communicates that you're listening carefully and are willing to learn a new language.

Speaking the language of the individual means figuring out what that language is. For example, does your partner scatter highly technical terms throughout conversations or does she fill them with management theory jargon? Perhaps she favors simplicity and brevity over complexity and long-windedness. You may be partnering with someone who gets right to the point and can't stand the common courtesies and other preamble activity that many people engage in.

Observe and adapt. This doesn't mean that you should adopt a communication style that is completely foreign to you or engage in one-sided conversations (where you're always listening and your partner is always talking). But be sufficiently flexible to adjust your usual style to some extent. For instance, your partner may be the type who likes to communicate information in a rush of words and without interruption. If this is the case, you may have to refrain from your usual tendency to interrupt with questions. All this is a small price to pay for building a deeper and more powerful Networlding connection.

Do You Validate Your Partner Through Your Listening?

It's difficult to develop trust in relationships unless people practice active listening. In passive listening, you sit there and absorb rather than respond. As a result, the speaker never truly feels that what he's saying is important or making an impact; there's a hollow feeling after he's said what's on his mind. In contrast, active listening shows you are fully focused on the meaning of what you are hearing, and your goal is to make sure you understand. Active listening looks like you are fully present—body leaning forward, eyes attentive (but not staring), and head occasionally nodding to indicate understanding and interest. You respond with questions and comments that demonstrate that you've been paying attention and that you've been affected by what's been said.

Do You Believe That Your Communication Is Roughly Equal?

In other words, do you feel that there is a good balance of listening and talking, of ideas and information, of questions and commentary? If you feel communication is too one-sided in any way, you need to address this issue with your partner and attempt to correct it. Unbalanced communication will ultimately create friction: the constant talker feels as if he's doing all the work, the idea-person feels as if she's the only creative one, and so on.

You don't need to strive for perfect equality. It may be that communication is unbalanced in certain areas but the sum total is balanced. By this we mean that one person may supply most of the ideas in conversation but the other person supplies most of the information.

Have You Established Comfortable Ways of Staying Connected?

In today's interconnected world there are many communication channels: e-mail, intranet, extranet, and Internet; voice mail, fax, letter, phone; and one-on-one meetings. People develop preferences both for channels of communication and for forums within these channels. One person may love meeting for lunch, another meeting in an Internet chat room. Your job as a networlder is to figure out where you'll both feel comfortable talking.

Jane found out that one of her partners, George, really didn't like getting voice mail messages. He was on the road frequently but would avoid reconnecting with Jane because he had an aversion (a somewhat neurotic one) to voice mail. After asking George if he had any suggestions about how she could stay in better touch with him, he suggested e-mail. She tried it and was amazed that George not only responded promptly to her e-mail messages but sent her messages frequently. She had found the right medium for their communication.

Enjoying Equal-Opportunity Relationships

Although opportunities may be difficult to come by in the initiating stage of networld relationships, they become more plentiful as relationships evolve. As both people become more comfortable with each other and more willing to extend their trust, they're more likely to share opportunities. For many of you, the notion of consciously developing and sharing opportunities may seem foreign. In the past, this was probably an unconscious response rather than something you pursued in an organized, highly intentional manner. In the next chapter, we'll be focusing on creating opportunities together in a fully mature Networlding relationship. Before you get to that point, however, you should have some experience with Networlding opportunities. Here are a few techniques that will help you gain this experience.

Identify the Opportunities

Opportunities surround you and your Networlding partner. The trick is to flush them out into the open. At first, this may prove challenging. It may appear as if all the good projects and people you want to become involved with are too far removed from you and your partner. Don't believe it. As we emphasized earlier, you're connected to people and possibilities but they're not immediately visible. Together with your partner ask the following questions in order to identify opportunities that are within your reach:

- What has been the hot topic of discussion between you and your partner or in your Networlding circles? Whatever topic is creating a great deal of discussion and is on everyone's minds, that topic holds opportunity potential.
- Do you know who has influence in the area of that topic? If neither of you knows this influencer, who else in your networld might? The odds are you can find someone who can

introduce you to this influencer for a discussion of possible opportunities.

- Can you find people who are influencers in this area by reading local or trade publications relevant to the topic? Just reading a relevant trade publication or doing an Internet search will yield the names of certain people who are obvious influencers. You can write to them directly or explore possible connections through your networld circles.

- Is there an opportunity that you wish existed but doesn't seem to be there? Missed opportunities are simply ones you weren't aware of. Just talking about a wished-for opportunity with your Networlding partner can yield all sorts of possibilities. It may be that your partner has some leads to give you or some ideas that may produce leads. It's also possible that talking about an opportunity can make it more real.

Jack, a copywriter in an ad agency, began talking to his Networlding partner about how much he wanted to write movies in Hollywood. This was a long-cherished dream and Jack had written a dozen scripts that he'd sent off to agents and producers, only to be rejected. Unbeknownst to Jack, his partner—a writer at another ad agency—had the same dream. They agreed that they'd begin asking around to see if they could find anyone they knew who might refer them to an agent. A week later, both Jack and his partner each discovered the same name—someone who had helped others in their midwestern city land agents in Los Angeles. Though they haven't yet written a movie, they've had the opportunity to work on some television shows and are moving in the right direction.

The opportunities you can create depend on your ability to influence, as Figure 7.1 illustrates.

We've already stated that there are a number of ways to influence others. Networlders rely on the ability to influence to achieve their goals. The opportunities you create depend both on what you want and what you can influence others to help you get, and to help them get. The best way networlders influence, however, is by making connections. By this we mean connecting one person to another and to opportunities. Networlders are constantly exploring the intersection of people and opportunities. This draws the attention of

Figure 7.1. How We Influence Others.

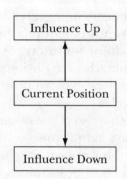

For example, decision makers: executives, industry leaders, community leaders, and so on.

For example, the people who influence decision makers: executive assistants, friends, colleagues of decision makers.

all participants in your networld as they observe your powerful ability to create.

Turn Obstacles into Opportunities

The old saying "When one door closes, another door opens" applies here. Too often, we feel sorry for ourselves when we lose a job or fail at a business deal, and others express sympathy. In fact, these obstacles are catalysts for exploring new people, situations, jobs, careers, and businesses. They can produce tremendous amounts of positive energy and fuel a search for new opportunities. When you encounter an obstacle, use it as an opportunity to talk to people in your networld about it and see if they have any ideas or leads to help you rebound. In most cases, networlders are eager to help partners who face obstacles and will work overtime to come up with a useful piece of information or connection. The following story illustrates how this process works.

When David found out that he was losing his job as a result of his company merging with its top competitor he looked to his primary circle for support. He found that George, a member of his networld, had lost his job under similar circumstances a year earlier. David asked George for assistance, and George referred David to Angela, who was an executive recruiter for a large executive search firm. Although David was not in an executive position, Angela took the time to give him job-search tips and the names of a couple of people to contact for potential jobs. Within three months David was working again. When he made his regular monthly phone call to George, he was asked if he had spoken to Angela recently. George emphasized the importance of staying in contact with people like Angela who are constantly meeting new people and connecting them with others, while also providing advice on how to develop mutually beneficial opportunities from the connections.

David took George's advice and placed Angela in his primary circle. After he was promoted to manager of his manufacturing division, Angela helped him negotiate a better salary and benefits package. During the following year David's company was in need of a new chief financial officer, and he recommended Angela's company for the search. Angela worked on the assignment and found a CFO who was a great fit.

A few years later David was frustrated because there was no opportunity for advancement at his company. Faced with this obstacle, he called Angela, who immediately thought of a company that was just planning to open up a new division and was looking for someone with David's qualifications. She recommended David and he eventually was hired for this plum position.

The point here is that opportunities don't always look like opportunities, and you need to talk about your obstacles with fellow networlders or they'll just remain obstacles.

Exchange Wisdom Support

As you nurture ongoing exchanges, you evolve the relationship to a new level, one where wisdom can be exchanged. It creates an environment of caring and compassion in all your exchanges. When we weave wisdom into our relationships, we achieve a higher quality of conversation. Whereas the knowledge exchange involves sharing our experience, wisdom is even deeper. It adds a spiritual side of ourselves. It is a combination of good judgment, common sense, and spirit. As a result of wisdom exchanges, we share more intimately about ourselves. This exchange creates even more trust, where we share our life's purpose. We and our Networlding partners become coaches for one another, helping realize each other's purpose.

Offering support through wisdom is a tougher exchange because you may find yourself having to say things people don't necessarily want to hear. Lori provides a good example. She was working at a job that was very exciting but not a good match for her skills. She used her networld for lots of emotional support exchanges where she poured out her frustration about how much her job drained her energy. One day, James, one of her networld partners, said, "Lori, are you open to me offering you some advice?" Lori was surprised by the change in his tone, and sat up to listen more closely before replying softly, "Sure, go ahead." James proceeded to talk candidly. He suggested that Lori leave her current job now before it got even harder for her. This, of course, was not at all what Lori wanted to hear, but she listened anyway because she had trust in their relationship and knew that James had no ulterior motives. They ended the conversation with Lori agreeing that she would think about her situation by herself during a quiet time away from the office, as he recommended.

Within two weeks Lori came to realize that the advice James offered was right. She *did* need to leave. His words helped her become more aware of her feelings and how she was not paying enough attention to them. Because her job was not fulfilling, she had little energy left to enjoy the personal side of her life. If she continued as she had been, she would not change things for the better. Her situation would just grow worse. Once she accepted it, she developed a plan to seek new employment. With James's help she found herself employed by someone in his secondary circle who was head of a nonprofit in less than sixty days. She also found that she had more energy and was now working in a field where she felt a calling.

Lori in turn sought to help James. She observed that he was always talking about wanting more meaningful work. He enjoyed his job, but something was missing. Lori advised James to look at training in his own company. Here, he could be more involved with teaching others, something that he had mentioned he loved doing earlier in life when he was a Sunday school teacher. James took Lori's advice and today finds himself very satisfied training others in his company's in-house sales training program.

Understanding that the nature of an exchange is to give back something, Lori started to offer more advice to James. She was a good writer, and these were skills that James lacked. She offered to help him develop his skills, and as a result James started receiving more recognition for his projects because his ideas were now communicated more effectively.

Create Transformational Opportunities Together

This is one of the top aims of Networlding (see again the support exchange model shown in Chapters One and Six), and one that we will talk more about in the next chapter. For now, we want you to recognize that you don't have to limit your opportunities to "small" stuff—a job interview, a minor business deal, a chance to attend a new seminar or conference. We know hundreds of networlders who have helped each other gain access to transformational opportunities. These opportunities can involve everything from discovering a rewarding new career to landing a huge client to partnering with a group in a fast-track business start-up.

Many people impose artificial limits on their opportunities. They convince themselves that what a Networlding partner suggests is impossible or that a discussion is just wishful thinking. Networlding gives people the human resources necessary to achieve the most ambitious goals, as the following story suggests.

Martha was tired of working for other people. After she received her MBA, she'd spent five years working for three different companies in the fashion industry. She'd done well and had a nice position and salary with her present employer, but she wasn't energized by the work. Louise, Martha's neighbor, had followed a related career path in retailing and left it to have children. Both her children were now in school and she had time on her hands. Martha and Louise were Networlding partners, and Louise had been especially empathic when Martha complained about office politics. In turn, Martha had given Louise emotional support when she expressed a desire to go back to work but wasn't sure if she'd be happy working for a large company.

One day Louise kiddingly suggested that since she and Martha obviously had no desire to work for anyone else, they should start their own company. After they laughed about it, they began taking the idea seriously. They realized that between the two of them, they had a significant amount of contacts at clothing stores throughout the country. Martha had another person in her primary circle—Jana, a young designer—who, she believed, had enormous talent but had been having trouble selling her designs to stores. Within a year, Martha and Louise set up a thriving business representing Jana and soon expanded it to include other talented young designers.

Opportunities help nurture and grow a relationship, and nurturing and growing a relationship leads to opportunities. You don't need to answer this chicken-or-egg question—neither the opportunity nor the nurturing has to come first. They occur simultaneously. When you concentrate on identifying opportunities, turning obstacles into opportunities, and seeking transformational opportunities, you naturally develop relationships in great ways. Working on opportunities together and helping others gain access to them is a rich, rewarding experience that produces mutual trust and respect. At the same time, if you focus on building this trust and respect and establishing deeper connections with those in your primary circle, opportunities are inevitable. Both you and your partner will be much more willing to exchange the various forms of support that lead to opportunities.

Build Community

When you are focused on nurturing relationships through ongoing exchanges, you realize that what you share with others creates a ripple effect that benefits many more than just yourself. In other words, there is every possibility that as you share with another and they share with another, and so on, you touch hundreds, perhaps thousands of people. As Jeff Bezos, president of Amazon.com, once commented, when someone doesn't like someone they don't just tell a few friends—they share their dissatisfaction with twenty thousand people in a newsgroup!

As we become more and more connected, what we share affects more and more people. Therefore, as you decide where you will place your energies in relationships, realize that you don't have to work as hard as you think to make a powerful difference for your networld partners and the many lives you will impact as your opportunities expand. This is the ultimate result of effective Networlding. More than ever, today we live in a world community. It is not unlikely, therefore, that your networld partners will reside in other parts of the world. An example is Barbara, who has two networld partners in Europe. Ian lives in Belgium, and Janet lives in London. Barbara met Janet via the Internet at an on-line community conference on knowledge sharing. Ian and Barbara met at a knowledge sharing conference in Boston. Both partnerships have evolved into new business opportunities that involve internal mentoring. The partners all see their involvement as a catalyst for growing new leaders in their respective organizations. In other words, they see the ripple effect of their exchanges helping others grow their careers. They see how their relationships have created transformational opportunities that will be transferred to the community at large.

Be Proactive

As we've already stated, networkers are more reactive than proactive, and some networlders display this tendency when initiating relationships. If you want a relationship to grow, however, you need to reverse this approach. Think about the power of promotional support. If you are regularly promoting those in your primary circle by sending out e-mails mentioning them or referring to them in your conversations, you are being proactive and should look for the same promotion in return. If you find that your partners remain reactive, try priming the pump with information about yourself that they can promote, such as a new job, an exciting project, an award received, an article published, or a speech given.

Being proactive means taking the initiative no matter how much you are disillusioned by others who should take the lead but don't. Many people sit back and wait for things to happen for them. They say things like, "It isn't fair that I have to be the one to manage everything or get everyone together." Rather than be resentful, recognize that if you initiate projects and do more than your fair share, you'll not only increase your chances of getting opportunities but you may stir your Networlding partner into action. We've found that networlders "wake up" when their partners are feeding them leads and ideas; an alarm goes off in their heads telling them it's time they reciprocate. When they do—when they start being proactive in the relationship—it naturally grows.

Proactivity can take many forms. Here are some things you might want to do to be more proactive:

- Consider one of your Networlding partner's goals and create a list of people you know who might help further these goals; ask your partner if he'd like you to refer him to them.
- Anticipate needs rather than wait to be asked. At this point in your Networlding relationship, you should be able to "read" your partner relatively well. Share ideas, information, emotional support, and people in anticipation of what you sense she requires.
- Mark down opportunities when they occur to you. You might hear about a job opening and think, "That would be perfect for Sue," or read about a new company opening a local office and realize that "Mark could help them set up their computer system." If you're not going to be in touch with Sue or Mark soon, write the information down to make sure you remember to pass it on when you next speak to them.
- Communicate potential opportunities regularly. They may turn out to be nothing, but if you make the effort your partners will always appreciate it. Doing so demonstrates that you are aware of what's important to them. Although you don't want to overwhelm them with trivial or irrelevant information, you also don't want to be proactive in this regard once in a blue moon.

Discovering the Magic of Connectivity

When networlders get on a roll—when their relationships mature and grow—they often talk about how they suddenly see all the hidden linkages to people and opportunities they never saw before. Networkers never experience this feeling; they only see the obvious connections. Networlders connect in highly creative ways that require creative thinking—bringing divergent ideas together to form a new and altogether unique opportunity. In essence, networlders use both sides of their brains when they create connections. Both the analytical side and the creative side come together when people network because they are making connections between what exists today and what could exist through the development of relationships.

Networlding invites people to make connections across traditional boundaries. You're no longer limited to your small circle of work or industry associates. Now you can tap into other sources, such as friends, relatives, people you meet at conferences, influencers who you would have never dared approach before. When you make a connection for a Networlding partner rather than for yourself, you cross another boundary. You become aware of the process of connecting as an objective observer, and you learn things you might have missed if you were more involved with the connection.

In many ways, Networlding is revelatory after connections are initiated, nurtured, and begin to pay dividends. Let's take Reid, for example, a young associate who worked at an accounting firm in Chicago where Melissa was consulting. When Melissa asked him to start Networlding, he wasn't certain if he could make any connections that would have much impact. After coaching, however, Reid began to see that he wasn't limited to the people he knew well—most of them young, recent college graduates like himself. Cognitively at least, he understood that connections spiral outward and upward in infinite circles.

Reid began initiating and then nurturing Networlding relationships. One of the relationships was with his girlfriend, who worked for a company that was looking for consulting services and products in the cost-recovery software area. He had a friend whose cousin worked for a growing consulting organization, who had the leading cost-recovery software in the marketplace. By linking his friend's cousin with his girlfriend's company, he drew attention to his Networlding abilities. The management of both companies took notice and started discussions about new job opportunities for Reid.

Reid was at first astonished by what his Networlding produced; then he was energized. He started nurturing and growing relationships in earnest. In the next month he landed two new clients for his firm through an unlikely series of connections (one involved his barber; another a former college professor whom he ran into in a restaurant).

Making connections is a highly creative process, one that requires being open to different possibilities and rejecting traditional assumptions. Reid had no way of knowing that his barber would lead him to a piece of business, but his openness to that possibility allowed it to happen. As you nurture and grow relationships, you'll find that all sorts of creative connecting possibilities present themselves. Your partner will hook you up with an unlikely source and you'll do likewise for your partner. When an opportunity develops from this connection, you'll find it that much easier to be innovative and open to other atypical connections.

The Networlding support exchange model is crucial to building a networld. If you integrate the seven support levels into each exchange you have with your networld partners, you will find yourself building a networld very quickly. We will revisit elements of the model during the next chapters to show you how to use it in an ongoing manner.

In the next chapter, you will learn how to create transformational opportunities together with your networld partners so that you both benefit. This is yet another level you can reach when you networld.

CHAPTER EIGHT

Step Six: Co-create Opportunities

Creating opportunities together means that two Networlding partners expand their Networlding to new levels by leveraging their combined talent. Although you and your partner may have brought opportunities to each other during the initiating and growth phases of your relationship, joint opportunities are more likely to occur when the relationship reaches a certain level of maturity. This is especially true if you're creating transformational opportunities together.

This kind of "co-creating" can take many forms. It may involve more formal relationships, like strategic alliances, or less formal ones, like project collaborations. Companies like General Electric have become champions of this connected model of organizational growth, using the term *boundaryless selling* to convey the message that everyone can work together, together creating opportunities for one another.

Moving from talk to action is what this is all about, as Larry and John discovered. Larry was a commodities trader on the New York Stock Exchange. His friend John was a top sales representative with a large Internet company in Connecticut. They had been friends since college and each year always took a different adventure vacation together. It was part of their pact with one another—a way of keeping in touch. Each year the two friends would also discuss their dream of opening an adventure travel service. After going through a Networlding workshop they decided that they had waited long enough. They committed to getting a plan together and started their own company that spring; it has now been going strong for three years.

Co-creating is a process; it's not something that just happens. Networlders learn that they need to follow certain guidelines in order to collaborate on opportunities that are significant, that not only result in financial success but also elevate their stature in an industry. These opportunities may be career-changing or even life-changing. Although it's possible to generate these opportunities by sitting down with someone and moving forward without a process, such an approach is usually ineffective. That kind of creation exists only on one level; the two people don't exchange the type of support that maximizes the opportunity. Ideas aren't exchanged that can turn a good opportunity into a great one. Emotional support isn't offered that can sustain the partnership through the rough initial stages of a project.

But before discussing the guidelines that lead to true co-creating, let's look at the different types of opportunities networlders commonly pursue.

Types of Networlding Opportunities

Networlders frequently co-create new business opportunities. Through their exchanges of knowledge and ideas and their interactions with other networlders, they recognize a golden opportunity to start a new company. Their advantage over others who decide to do the same thing has a lot to do with their shared values; they are unlikely to break apart a few months or years because they suddenly find out that their belief systems are in opposition. They are focused on how to help each other to achieve a shared gain. They also possess an edge in the regularity and diversity of their knowledge exchanges; they partner in an intellectually dynamic way, founding companies on information and ideas rather than only a business plan and money. And third, they're well connected; they have access to a wide variety of resources in their respective networlds to help the business grow.

Opportunities may also involve "other-directed" projects. For instance, many people in organizations are partnering to establish support groups for women and minorities. AT&T, IBM, and Baxter all have groups that help women and minorities grow professionally. Two people in an organization that lacks this kind of group might form one or launch a project in conjunction with an existing group. We've known a number of networlders who have together created community outreach programs or launched not-for-profit associations related to their jobs or supported by business organizations. Here the opportunities are to help others, but the networlders also benefit because they meet influencers and add to their primary circles. In a very real sense, the opportunity is also to interact with people they might never encounter in typical work situations.

Knowledge-sharing groups are another forum for Networlding opportunities. Organizations such as Sweden's Erickson have facilitated knowledge sharing by linking their seventeen thousand employees through a computer network in forty research centers in twenty countries. Arthur Andersen's Knowledge Space is a similar knowledge-sharing environment where both employees and the public can share cutting-edge thought leadership on a wide variety of topics. Organization-sponsored knowledge exchange sites offer networlders an alternative way to co-create. They may find a Networlding partner halfway around the world who shares their values and goals. Many people—especially younger people—feel very comfortable exchanging knowledge, ideas, and even emotional support on-line. Companies encourage this exchange in the belief that it will result in fresh ideas and problem-solving practices.

Now and especially in the future, people will create together increasingly through electronic environments. This fact is already recognized by Networlding organizations that set up intranet and extranet structures to connect people internally with their coworkers as well as externally with their suppliers and customers. With the blessing of corporate employers and the tools and techniques provided to facilitate exchanges, these electronic forums will give networlders instant access to their partners.

Acting on Joint Opportunities

No matter how or where opportunities are co-created, the process remains relatively constant. Let's look at the ten guidelines networlders use to find and act on these opportunities.

Analyze Complementary Strengths

Networlders don't co-create joint opportunities with mirror images of themselves. They recognize that creativity springs from differences more than similarities—not differences in values or goals but in skills and knowledge. Opportunities emerge when two people with different strengths but shared objectives bring their thoughts to bear on a problem or situation. Sparks are created through friction. Someone who is skilled at sales challenges a financial person's perspective on a potential project. The financial person comes back and articulates his own spin on the salesperson's idea. From this dynamic, new concepts emerge that are original and energized. Although the two perspectives may clash at times, they ultimately are complementary, and this is how opportunities are found.

Sit down with a Networlding partner, analyze your individual strengths, and determine if they're complementary. What is the one thing you do better than most? What is the one thing your partner does better? If you're both talented at the same skills or in the same area, this can be problematic when it comes to creating joint opportunities. You're going to be duplicating each other rather than blending skills and pushing each other in new directions. It may be that if you want to work on an opportunity together, you'll need to bring in another Networlding partner who has a complementary strength. Remember too that your complementary strengths don't have to be obvious core competencies, such as finance or sales. One of you may be terrific at thinking outside of the box; the other may be the type of person who knows how to get things done.

Ideally, your co-creating experience will be similar to that of Jonas and Andrea. Jonas ran a hearing and speech clinic. He had been very successful for more than twelve years, but now work was tougher; he couldn't find the skilled employees he needed to support his efforts and he was worried about the business's future. Although his bottom line continued to look good, he knew that it was only a matter of time before it suffered. Jonas turned to his networld for support. He talked with Andrea, an accountant he had developed a special relationship with—someone he thought would be a good partner with whom to co-create. Andrea and Jonas spent a couple of hours over the course of two weeks talking about their complementary skills. Andrea had worked for the same organization over the last ten years and although she had become a partner in the firm, she found that the work was not fulfilling her values: she believed in doing things that made a difference for other people. Her job didn't have much people contact to begin with, and that contact was lessening.

Jonas's interest in creating an opportunity together with someone else had come at the right time for Andrea. She had a decent amount of money already set aside for retirement and some additional savings for a rainy day. She and Jonas talked about many options—starting a new business, collaborating on a seminar in healthy living they could both teach on weekends, and running Jonas's clinic together. They finally agreed that their passions and the present opportunity to grow Jonas's clinic was the best option. Andrea, who had great organizational skills, took over the clinic's day-to-day administration. This freed up Jonas to write some articles on new techniques he had been pioneering for speech and hearing—his strength. As a result of these articles, Jonas was contacted by a few professional medical associations and asked to give talks on his new techniques. As a result of his speeches, he received more requests for speaking, and eventually a great deal of additional business.

Share Intentions

The second step of the process is one that many networkers fail to take. Or rather, they don't take it fully, feeling as if they must hide some or most of their intentions from the people in their networks. Their fear is that someone else will "steal" their ideas. They also worry that someone will tear down their concept and rob them of the energy and initiative they need to make it happen.

Sharing intentions is an act of faith; it assumes that your Networlding partner will respond to your intentions fairly, constructively, and honestly. No matter how well you know someone or how much that person's values and objectives seem to mirror your own, there's an element of risk involved. At the same time, sharing intentions catalyzes an exchange from which opportunities emerge and are developed jointly with your Networlding partner.

You may share your intention to do many things, including these: quit your job and find a new one, change careers, stop working for others and start working for yourself, create a new product or service, look for a business partner, acquire an organization, take a business in a new direction, propose an innovative strategy to your boss, move to a new location and start a business there.

Sharing these intentions sparks dialogue. When you reveal your plans, you encourage your partners to comment and become

involved. Being completely honest and forthright about your intentions will stimulate others to contribute, and their contributions
can enhance your idea and lead to other, better ideas.

Connecting students with the business community has been
Chris Genzler's intention for the last four years. His profession as a
certified financial planner led him in 1995 to the Oak Brook, Illinois, Association of Commerce and Industry (OBACI), where he
became actively involved in the leadership development committee. Chris also wanted to make a difference in his community,
specifically helping young people. He strongly believed that providing students with exposure to different careers before college
was crucial for both students and businesses, and he decided he
wanted to find a way to turn this idea into a program.

In 1997, Chris shared his intention to do this with a couple of
key Networlding partners at OBACI. His willingness to advocate
for this idea and his fervent belief in it led to a number of highly
productive discussions with his Networlding partners. As a result
of these discussions, they eventually set up the Education to
Careers subcommittee. Within a year the group grew to involve five
area high schools and dozens of students. These students were
introduced regularly to local businesspeople and given a chance
to learn about professions and organizations that interested them.
The group has now formed a leadership development program in
which they are partnering with local colleges.

By being clear and convincing about his intentions, Chris was
able to create opportunities not only for students but for himself as
well. His expressed intention of helping young people discover
careers galvanized others in his networld into action, and the result
has been a flourishing program that has given hundreds of students
an exposure to work environments that they probably would never
have had otherwise. At the same time, Chris was invited to be on
the OBACI board of directors and a member of the steering committee for DuPage Area Education to Careers initiative. As a result
of this involvement, Chris has met a wide variety of influencers and
professionals from business and educational fields, which has
afforded him opportunities to obtain new financial planning clients.
A cross-pollination occurred: Chris' financial planning clients
became involved in the Education to Careers program and his Education to Careers contacts became financial planning clients.

Articulate and Analyze Opportunities

Networlders aren't shy about examining opportunities from all angles. They feel free to poke and prod an opportunity in order to co-create the best possible scenario. The articulation and analysis step requires a significant amount of openness and a lack of defensiveness. Networlders don't talk about opportunities just to impress other people, and they feel sufficiently comfortable with their partners to point out flaws. Opportunities emanate from values and beliefs, and as such they aren't taken lightly or cynically. Although there are many ways to talk about opportunities, we've found that when Networlding partners center the discussion around the following questions, they are more likely to come up with a joint opportunity:

- What one opportunity do we hope to develop within the next three months?
- How does this opportunity help us achieve our goals?
- How does this opportunity reflect our values?
- What types of resources do we need to take full advantage of the opportunity?
- Who are all the people or organizations that could be involved with the opportunity?
- What first steps do we need to take to initiate this opportunity; who else in our networld might prove to be of assistance?
- What roadblocks might hamper this opportunity from developing; what creative solutions can we come up with to address these roadblocks?

As you discuss your answers, pay attention to disconnects. Most obviously, determine if your Networlding partner is buying into or shying away from the opportunity as you analyze it. If you reveal a major roadblock, talk about whether you are realistic in thinking you can get around it. If you see a value problem, don't try and rationalize it away; networlders don't pursue opportunities that clash with their values. Frank, perceptive conversations with other networlders about opportunities help the best ones spring to life and the worst ones fade away without your wasting a great deal of time and money on them.

Darion and Vivian answered these questions before they co-created a Web site together. Darion, a graphic artist, talked at length with Vivian, a commercial printer, about the opportunity to codevelop a site that would showcase both of their businesses. During their initial discussions, they agreed that this venture satisfied both their values and goals, but they also found that they lacked a resource that would be essential in making the site successful. Reluctantly, they agreed that it was unrealistic for them to do all the site management necessary; they didn't have the time or talent for this task. As a result, they made the commitment to hire an administrative assistant who would be responsible for developing the traffic on the site and turning that traffic into customers for both companies. Vivian and Darion also identified potential roadblocks. For instance, both of them foresaw problems with measuring the success of this opportunity; they worked long and hard at developing measures (number of visits and amount of "purchases") that would indicate whether the site was an effective business tool for both of them, thus avoiding potential disagreements down the road.

After six months, Darion and Vivian agreed that their co-created site was a huge success. They were surpassing their mutual goals and finding that their analysis paid off, and they were so well prepared for problems and so well matched in what they wanted the site to achieve that the opportunity grew faster and more significantly than they had thought possible.

Practice Reciprocity

This may seem obvious, but reciprocity often becomes lost when an individual single-mindedly focuses on an opportunity. It may be that a Networlding partner benefits from the opportunity as much as you do; in that case, reciprocity is a given. In other instances, however, one individual doesn't benefit directly or as much as the other; for example, you ask a partner for a referral or to put his financial skills to use to determine the viability of a new business.

Without reciprocity, Networlding relationships collapse. In its absence, there is resentment instead. The relationship is undermined even if an opportunity is created because one person is getting more out of it than the other. Therefore, do everything you can to maintain equal-opportunity relationships.

When we hold Networlding events for organizations, we stress reciprocity. Organizational managers are usually very good at many aspects of Networlding, but they sometimes think about using the people they partner with as resources rather than as equal participants in opportunities. Therefore, when we pair up people and start them co-creating opportunities, we make them toe the reciprocity line: they cannot create opportunities if there is no payback for the other person. This doesn't mean that each opportunity has to benefit both people equally, but it does mean that if one person benefits more than another from a given opportunity, that person will help the other with a pet project at some point in the near future.

Reciprocity imperatives can greatly enhance the quality of Networlding sessions. A large, progressive accounting firm decided to host a Networlding event that would include a law firm and a bank of equal size. Melissa was asked to host the event and help attendees learn how to create opportunities together. Given the three different areas of interest, it was logical to assume that co-creating opportunities would be a challenge; what represented an opportunity for the accounting firm might not be seen as an opportunity by lawyers or bankers, and vice versa. The reciprocity rule, however, was strictly enforced. As a result, a number of terrific opportunities for all three firms were produced.

Examine Cross-Selling Possibilities

Networlders don't view opportunities in the traditional, limited sense of the word. An opportunity isn't simply a "deal" between two partners that can be done now. You can extend an opportunity beyond the immediate relationship to other people in your or your partner's networld. The most common extension is cross-selling to one of your existing customers. This is not something most people do naturally. A hoarding mentality—based on a fear that someone will get more than we are getting—is common. People are naturally greedy with their clients and customers, and they don't readily introduce them to others. The fear is that if you introduce a client to someone and the relationship goes badly, it will negatively affect your own relationship. The equally strong but opposite fear is that such an introduction might result in your client leaving you to become your partner's client.

Although shared values and goals should create enough trust to minimize these fears, they are so powerful that they may still persist among networlders. It helps to talk about these issues with your partner and set some do's and don'ts regarding customers. By setting some parameters, you can then benefit from cross-selling. Customers often are a great addition to your primary circle; they are frequently influencers and people who need a well-defined group of products and services. In short, they are in a good position to create joint opportunities with you.

Sam, for instance, was a sales manager for a large corporation. His Networlding partner, Denise, owned a small software company. They'd known each other for years and had been in each other's primary circles for almost eighteen months. Still, Sam was hesitant about referring Denise to any of his major customers. As much as he trusted and respected Denise—and as willing as she was to refer her customers to him—he had difficulty taking this cross-selling step. Sam rationalized that his customers were much larger than Denise's and that he was taking a much larger risk than she was. At the same time, he knew that Denise could help at least one of his clients, who was experiencing great difficulty getting the bugs out of a new customer order software system and had even asked Sam if he knew anyone who could help the firm straighten the problem out.

Finally, Sam opened up to Denise about his concerns. Denise appreciated that he was being open about it and said that she had sensed his fears. They explored the worst-case scenario: she would mess up a job for one of Sam's customers. Sam agreed that because of Denise's expertise and a value she shared with Sam (accountability), this was not likely. But even if it did occur, they agreed, the odds were that there wouldn't be negative repercussions. Sam realized that most of his customers were reasonable people who would hold Denise responsible for her actions, not Sam. As a result of this discussion, Sam referred Denise to his customer with the software bugs, and Denise helped him fix the problem. Even better, Denise and this customer together created a great opportunity—they designed a new customer order system that the company then installed and that greatly accelerated the company response time. The customer was so grateful to Sam for referring Denise that he began sending more business Sam's way.

Form Strategic Alliances

We're often asked about *whom* people should partner with to co-create opportunities. After all, networlds stretch far and wide. Should you be purely opportunistic and partner with the person who is in the best position to develop a specific type of opportunity? Does it matter if the individual is in your primary, secondary, or tertiary circle?

As a general rule of thumb, it makes sense to concentrate on co-creating with people in your primary circle. They're the ones who have the influence and shared values you need to produce a positive collaborative effort. At the same time, however, not everyone in your primary circle will lead you to the types of opportunities you're looking for at a given time in your life. One person will help you achieve specific goals better than another (and vice versa). In other words, you want to create a *strategic alliance*.

Strategic alliances are relationships you form to focus on targeted opportunities. Even when companies form alliances, the reality is that the core of the alliance is a relationship between two people (who are often called *relationship managers* or *alliance champions*). Alliances are strategic in the sense that they're planned with long-term and short-term goals in mind as well as resources required, tactics, and all the other elements of strategic planning. We've created a list of questions that will help you determine if co-creating with a given individual will result in a strategic alliance. You've already answered a few of the following questions, but others are new:

- Does the individual share your goals in creating opportunities? Does she want to pursue an opportunity that will further her career, make money, achieve an entrepreneurial dream, make a difference in the world, and so on? And does this match your motivation?
- Is the other person's strength complementary or redundant to your own and is it relevant or irrelevant to the type of opportunity you're interested in pursuing?
- Does your prospective co-creator have the influence necessary to help you achieve your opportunity objectives? Is she willing to use that influence on behalf of the opportunities you co-create?

- If this individual won't benefit as much as you will from this opportunity, are you in a position to help her achieve her goals for opportunities that are more beneficial to her?
- If you look at both your networld and your prospective partner's, do they reach the people and resources necessary to achieve your opportunity goals?

Create Mentoring Opportunities

As we've emphasized, networlders create opportunities together in all sorts of ways. They see opportunity not just in financial gain but in experiences that add depth and meaning to their lives. Mentoring, for instance, is an integral part of Networlding. Over the last decade we have mentored dozens of people, and our fulfillment has come in the form of appreciation from those we have mentored as well as in rich new learning experiences for ourselves.

As we have emphasized, giving and receiving is the underlying dynamic of Networlding, and mentoring allows this dynamic to play out in different but equally rewarding ways. Did you see the movie *Mr. Holland's Opus?* In it, the students of the title character, who has been a music teacher for many years, return to honor him. One of the students has since become governor of the state. She pays tribute to Mr. Holland by declaring that the real symphony he has created over the years is made up of his students, who are testimonies to his talents. In other words, Mr. Holland is a mentor.

In every job and in every career, there are times when we work at tasks that seem meaningless or boring; nothing is given or received. Although it's important to imbue work with as much significance as possible, sometimes work provides a relatively small amount of satisfaction and we need to look elsewhere for sustenance. For anyone who has achieved a certain level of expertise or knowledge in a job, there's the opportunity for a rewarding exchange—giving some of that hard-won knowledge in exchange for respect and gratitude.

One young man named Scott was particularly appreciative of the wisdom his mentor exchanged with him and asked what he could do in return for the support. His mentor looked at him and said simply, "Give back to me by becoming a great leader—the kind of leader that values and empowers other lives as you feel I have done for you." Scott has made this his goal and has committed to mentoring others as he gains the requisite experience and expertise.

Many ways exist for you to create opportunities with another individual through mentoring. The simplest involves finding a young person in your office who shares your goals and values and forge a partnership that goes beyond the traditional supervisor–direct report relationship. You may also decide to participate in a more formal mentoring program. Or you could start such a program with a Networlding partner to help young people in a specific field, school, or situation.

In one sense, the reciprocity of Networlding is absent from mentoring relationships because the older, more experienced person has more to give than the younger, less experienced individual. In another sense, however, reciprocity does exist because mentors frequently say that what they receive from these experiences goes beyond intangible (though important) feelings of contributing to another's growth. Many mentors explain that those under their tutelage provide insights and information that they would never have learned about from the people they usually associate with. As managers, they gain insights into the dreams and concerns of young people in their organization; this helps them be better managers. Mentors also become more self-aware from the feedback of those they coach; they gain a new understanding of how they come across to a different group of people. Mentors have also told us that those they coached have hopped on the fast track and quickly attained positions of influence where they could work together to create opportunities as equal Networlding partners. In this sense, they have seeded relationships that may blossom into part of their growing networld.

Bridge Divergent Networlds

Co-creating also means constantly locating new people with similar values from diverse backgrounds. Bridging divergent networlds allows you access to more diverse opportunities. Rather than creating new projects and concepts with the same group of people— resulting in the same types of opportunities—networlders connect with people from different fields, of different ages, from different countries, and so on. We know one young networlder whose primary circle includes people from three different countries. Another net-worlder, an accountant, has been recruited by someone in his pri-mary circle to be part of a team attempting to build a skyscraper in a Third World country. Still another networlder, a former CEO of a midsize company, was able to make the transition to executive director of a not-for-profit association because he bridged diver-gent networlds.

If you're not making a conscious effort to bridge networlds, it probably won't happen. People tend to run in redundant circles. This means they continue to connect with the same people over pro-longed periods of time, sometimes over a lifetime. In a world where unrelenting innovation is necessary, redundant networkers are left behind. We are creatures of habit who become accustomed to those who do as we do. The phrase "birds of a feather flock together" describes this habit. Go to a chamber of commerce meeting and you'll see how true this is: all the bankers or accountants, for exam-ple, are sitting with their professional colleagues at one table.

To bridge divergent networlds and expand the range of oppor-tunities you can create with others, try the following:

- Join clubs, associations, or other groups that are organized not by profession but by some interest that encourages diversity; these groups might include civic organizations, political com-mittees, not-for-profit volunteer groups, and so on.
- Ask others in your networld if you can accompany them to a meeting, seminar, or conference where the people are from different professions or have different interests or ethnicity than yours.
- Connect with family members and friends who might provide you with an introduction to individuals or groups who are sig-nificantly different from the people you usually associate with.
- Use joint opportunities created with a Networlding partner as "recruiting" tools to bring in people with divergent skills and knowledge in pursuit of your common goal; reverse the usual order of things and use the opportunity as a magnet for diverse individuals.

Alan used this last approach when he began his Internet com-pany. He was seeking "angel" investment financing to build a company that was focused on creating a portal, like Yahoo, for car buying. While on vacation with his wife in Amsterdam, he sent out a press release through one of his colleagues to two thousand media outlets that received press releases on-line. Within two days, even before he flew home, Alan was receiving requests from venture capitalists to invest in his company. He had articles appear in major newspapers and magazines. Throughout the next couple of months he brought people together with the focused opportunity of his new company and leveraged one influential relationship to achieve another. Broadcasting the opportunity gave Alan the exposure he needed to divergent networlds, and they helped him co-create his opportunity in ways he could only dream about before establishing these diverse connections.

Play with Opportunities

Networkers are very businesslike in their approach to opportunities; they think about them in linear fashion. We encourage you to be more conceptual and adventurous in your discussions. Don't settle for the opportunities at your fingertips. Of course, don't ignore the obvious, but also be sure to explore the less obvious. You can play with opportunities in a number of ways, including these:

Identify the Idea You're Working On and Create Variations on the Theme

For instance, if you are currently selling a product line to European countries, create a list of ten different groups that might also be interested in the product line. Or come up with five different strategies to sell it to these European countries. Or create three new marketing approaches that position the product line in fresh, exciting ways. The point is to spin projects or ideas around, to view them from fresh perspectives. This playful approach is a great way for you and a networld partner to talk about and expand on a mutual opportunity. It's also something you can do on your own to rethink who would be a good co-creating partner. Thinking about an opportunity in a new way often helps you make a mental connection to a partner in your networld; someone you never considered partnering with before suddenly seems like an obvious choice.

Vince Racioppo, president of the Center for Expert Performance in Highland Park, Illinois, had created an assessment tool for analyzing expert performance of top salespeople. Vince began playing with his assessment tool and discovered that there was no reason to limit it to salespeople. His list of other possible markets included marketing, customer service, and other areas, and he began adapting and expanding the tools his company offered. Now he also licenses his expert assessment tools to other groups, providing them with opportunities for new services and himself with an opportunity for increased profits (he receives a percentage as part of this licensing arrangement).

Identify Someone Else's Opportunity to See How You Might Contribute

Don't fall victim to the "not-invented-here" syndrome. Just because it wasn't your original idea doesn't mean that you can't become a valuable nurturer of that idea. Think about projects and ventures that others in your networld have told you about. How might your skills and knowledge help these projects and ventures flourish?

Marilyn was an independent consultant and had had her own company for the last six years. She wanted to create new opportunities for business growth but hadn't been very successful with any of the growth opportunities she had pursued on her own. She put out the word to her networld that she was interested in hearing about people or organizations that were doing exciting work in the high-tech sector, a field in which she had some involvement but that was still tangential to her main consulting area. Within the next few weeks, she heard about four different high-tech ventures, one of them a start-up that had tremendous financing as well as a terrific product that seemed to ensure its success. But when Marilyn had lunch with the company's founder, he admitted that as technically skilled as he and others in the company were, no one had much business experience. Marilyn did, and she quickly became a valuable consultant. Their relationship produced the type of growth she was looking for: she received an equity stake in the company.

Use Provocative, Unexpected Questions to Push Opportunities Further

One Networlding pair, Liz and Tony, made it a yearly event to take a weekend and brainstorm new opportunities they could work together to create. Although they were both real estate professionals, their true love was gardening and that's what their ideas revolved around. One year they decided to create a series of booklets on gardening, and then sold them over the Internet. The next year they codeveloped a gardening shear; it has become a profitable product. Their ideas emerged from the questions they asked each other, including these: Would gardeners be willing to pay a little extra for top-quality manure, and would a catalogue of manure products appeal to gardeners frustrated with the inferior quality they buy at most retail outlets? What garden tool do you hate to use the most? Would gardeners be willing to design their gardens on a computer if the software made it easy to do? What's the most difficult flower to grow and what might we do to make it easier for people who want to grow it?

We're so quick to provide answers and so slow to ask questions. Yet questions allow us to be playful with ideas and push them in new directions. Networlders ask great, imaginative questions, and this helps them create great, imaginative opportunities.

Think Peripherally

When it comes to building new business and career opportunities, we all have blind spots. This is because we are usually too focused on the tasks we have at hand to see something right beside us or to realize that the people with whom we are connected are links and bridges to fresh opportunities.

Thinking peripherally leads to unexpected opportunities. As with Liz and Tony, the opportunities may not exist in your area of expertise or your business. If you and other networlders look beyond your daily routines (and divergent networlds facilitate peripheral thinking because they force people outside of their familiar, comfortable zones), you'll find new ideas and projects that currently seem beyond your reach.

For instance, Dan Dickinson is the owner of an airplane company called General Aviation Services. A terrific peripheral thinker, Dan talked to members of his networld and realized that he wasn't just in the airplane business. Or rather, he realized that being in the airplane business gave him leverage that he could use to get into seemingly unrelated businesses. With this thinking, he created a new company that sold electrical generators powered by refurbished World War II–era helicopter engines. Dan found that he could get these engines for half the cost that his competitors paid; furthermore, his people had the technical know-how to retrofit them for power plants in Third World countries that required a dependable, relatively low-cost power source for their plants.

Peripheral thinking requires looking sideways rather than straight ahead. It's a figurative turning of your head so that you can see how to adapt a skill, product, or service to a seemingly unrelated use. Here's another example. Ben worked for a five-star hotel in Washington, D.C. Ecology-minded and looking for opportunities to expand his career beyond the relatively menial job he had, he started thinking peripherally. He formed a networld relationship with one of the bellhops, Sam, and they started a hotel recycling program that worked so well they gained recognition from management. Within six months the two were put in charge of the entire hotel chain's recycling program, and they received nice promotions and raises.

Opportunities Are Like Snowflakes: No Two Are Exactly Alike

These ten guidelines will facilitate the co-creation process, but we could provide you with many more guidelines and still not cover the myriad opportunities and related requirements of each. As you can well imagine, starting a business from scratch with a Networlding partner is quite different from launching a new work team in your organization with advice from a few fellow networlders. A mentoring opportunity involves different types of people and issues than one where the goal is to change careers.

Nevertheless, your networld will be an invaluable resource for whatever opportunity you choose to pursue. Joint creation of opportunities in a networld context provides an abundance of ideas, information, emotional support, and influencers to draw upon. In many ways, the supply is inexhaustible because networld connections are dynamic and continuously changing, leading people to new people regularly.

To maximize your networld's ability to help you create opportunities with others, you must practice opportunistic behaviors in your networld interactions. This means saying and doing things that encourage others to co-create with you or lend support to the opportunities you're targeting. Refer to the following checklist:

Continuously Share Information About Your Abilities

As we've said before, this isn't about bragging or being self-centered. It's about making your networld aware of what your skills are so they can bring opportunities to you and understand what you bring to opportunities. Essentially, what you want to communicate is this: "I'm good at what I do and proud of the relationships I have developed. I'd like to share my talents and connections with you. In turn, I'd like you to share your talents and connections with me."

Treat Your Primary Circle Partners the Same Way as Prospects

When you've established a bond of trust with the people in your circle, you will find that you can ask just about anything of them (and they of you). If you have an opportunity, present it to them. One person will be eager to create it with you, whereas another will provide tremendous support. The key is to present it to your circle as if they were your best prospects. Treat them with respect and honesty and communicate with them regularly about opportunities. You can ask them, "Who else do you know who can help us with this?" and they will respond with great suggestions.

Ask For and Capitalize on Referrals from Your Primary Circle Partners

Never underestimate the power of your networld to deliver opportunities to your doorstep. But you can't be shy about it or only ask for help on special occasions. Networlding is a constant give and take, and you have to be prepared to do both. If you're interested in an opportunity, invite your primary circle to participate in its creation and development. When you do, you'll get better advice and higher-quality referrals than you could ever have imagined.

When Andrew was looking to develop a sales plan to market a new line of copiers that offered digital printing he made it known to his primary circle that his best referral would be to company purchasing agents, specifically companies with at least five hundred employees. Andrew's five primary circle partners provided him with seven top prospects. Andrew asked each of his partners to contact these prospects in advance, introduce the opportunity he was offering, and recommend they take the time to meet with him.

Andrew met with all seven prospects and acquired contracts with five of them. Rather than the traditional six- to twelve-month sales cycle, the time was reduced to less than two months. It took Andrew longer to set up meetings through his primary circle than it usually took to make cold calls. However, he made up for lost time as he met with prequalified prospects who were open to the opportunity he was offering. His primary circle partners successfully transferred their influence to Andrew, who in turn leveraged that influence to achieve his goals.

Assess the Influence of Your Primary Circle Members with Referrals

No matter what the opportunity might be, it's most likely to pan out if a person of high influence connects you to an influential individual. Let's say you're a young news reporter from Podunk, Iowa, and the opportunity you want to pursue is a career in network television news. Fortunately, Walter Cronkite happens to be in your primary circle. When he refers you to Dan Rather, you can count on him to be a great help in making your opportunity happen.

Therefore, assess your Networlding partner's influence with the person she's referring you to. Sometimes this is obvious. Other times, you may need to ask questions such as, "How do you know Mr. Rayburn?" and "Have you worked together in the past, and what did that work relationship entail?" You should also ask your fellow networlders to rate their influence with someone on a scale of one to five. This brings a quantitative measurement into a usually qualitative process, helping you plan a strategy for dealing with a referral. If influence is high, then you can expect a very positive interaction without any special effort on your part. If it's low, you're going to have to do more work to make the interaction one that will facilitate your opportunity.

Meet and Exceed the Opportunity Needs of Your Primary Circle Partners

Don't wait until someone helps you with an opportunity before you return the favor. Be proactive; volunteer information and ideas when people in your networld send out a call for assistance. If you meet your partners' needs, they will be that much more willing to meet yours. In fact, if you provide them with more assistance than they expect, they will bend over backwards to help you with your opportunities.

When Jerry mentioned to Steve that he was looking for a new position, Steve connected him to his friend Sarah. Sarah was happy to help Jerry, who was interested in transitioning into a career in the hotel industry. Sarah had been in this industry for more than fifteen years. She became a new primary partner for Jerry, referring him to several people in the industry who further shared with him their connections. Meanwhile, Steve kept up with Jerry and his progress and continued to support his job search. Within two months Jerry found himself employed by a new hotel in a management trainee position. Steve and Sarah continued to support Jerry, recommending that their trade associations hold their monthly meetings at the hotel. As Jerry's career evolved and he became an influencer, he was extraordinarily attuned to both Steve's and Sarah's opportunity requirements. Whenever either of them put out the word that they needed something, Jerry was the first one to contact them and offer ideas, referrals, and support.

Demonstrate Energy and Commitment

To put this in negative terms: don't be a "slug" and don't be a fair-weather partner. Networlding requires energy, and it demands continuous communication and vigorous pursuit of opportunities. If you're lazy, network. If you're willing to work overtime to connect with a diverse group of people and forge deep, meaningful relationships, networld. Co-creating opportunities is something that high-energy people do.

These people are also willing to make a commitment to an opportunity. They don't back out at the first sign of trouble or withdraw support when something better comes along. They make a commitment to their primary circle partners, demonstrating a dogged determination to bring an opportunity to fruition. Commitment has an almost magical effect on opportunity. People who are strongly committed to a project seem to benefit from the guidance of an "invisible hand." Charles Lindbergh put it best: "When I am committed, everything falls into place. Unforeseen forces come forth to support me."

As you move through the continuous process of exchanging and jointly creating opportunities with your networld partners you may come to the point where you know you need to change a relationship. For example, you no longer hold the same passions or interests. In the next chapter we will share with you a way to deal with this situation that is often not easy but necessary to continuing on the path of the networlder.

CHAPTER NINE

Step Seven: Re-create Your Networld

Networlds and the relationships they hold are dynamic rather than static. As a result, they need continuous monitoring, assessment, and reformulation. Because of all the opportunities you and your partners co-create, all of you will change. New opportunities will lead to new jobs, careers, and businesses. In both your personal and professional lives, you'll experience growth. The connections that proved so important at one point in your life will no longer be as important. Other connections that seemed relatively minor will become major. New people will join your networld and veteran partners will leave. There will be a back-and-forth movement of people in your primary, secondary, and tertiary circles.

Because there is so much flux, it's important not to take a networld for granted. Although you may create opportunities together with some partners for years, others will no longer be good partners for you (or you for them). Awareness of what's taking place in your networld and a willingness to respond quickly to maintain its high level of effectiveness is crucial.

Thus, the seventh step is about keeping on top of developments in your networld and using this awareness to re-create it (and your place in it).

Reassess Your Goals, Mission, and Values

Goals, missions, and values change, and when they do you need to re-create your networld in ways that dovetail with your new view of these guiding lights. Too many people, however, aren't particularly conscious when their goals, mission, or values change. In the back of their mind, they may recognize that they're dissatisfied with their current job or career or that they no longer value certain things (such as making money) as much as they once did, but they aren't willing to admit that the concepts that have shaped their lives up to this point are no longer viable.

Talk to people in your primary circle about your goals, mission, and values (and theirs). Be honest if you suspect that the ones you wrote down at the beginning of the process are no longer working for you. There's no secret to knowing when a goal has ceased to function for you. It's a matter of measuring your passion for it. At one point in your life, you were driven to achieve something. If that passion is absent—if the goal is only moderately important to you or unimportant—you need to redefine what it is you're seeking. The same is true if a value feels wrong or if your instincts tell you your mission has changed. When you redefine one or all of these things, you inevitably require new networld partners.

Back in Chapter Three (Step One) we talked about designing your mission, values, and vision. Maintaining relationships requires us to revisit continually these foundational pieces of our life plan to reach our goals and realize our full potential.

Evelyn learned she needed to reevaluate her goals when each work day seemed to last a week. When she was seventeen, she told everyone that all she ever wanted was to be a corporate attorney. So when she landed a plum position as an attorney for a prestigious clothing manufacturer, she felt she had it made. Evelyn spent the next ten years working her way up to general counsel.

Evelyn also became very involved with her local bar association, writing articles on her area of expertise: copyright infringement. She was recognized by her peers as one of the best in her field and paid commensurately. But then she started feeling disconnected from her work. She spent her spare time leafing through magazines that pictured log homes, thinking about how she would like to live in the country and raise her two girls, now ages seven and three, in a quieter, small-town environment.

Evelyn had been a widow for the last two years—her husband had passed on from cancer, a tragedy that she now realized brought her to the realization that no one can count on tomorrow.

Her husband's insurance policy had left her with a nest egg and she had some savings, but in all it wouldn't be enough to sustain the family longer than about a year. Being very practical, Evelyn didn't know what type of work she could do to make the kind of money she and her children would require.

When she sat down and reevaluated her goals, she realized that what really excited her was writing. She'd gotten increasing satisfaction from her legal writing, and she'd done some other writing projects—an op-ed piece, an article for the women's section of the local newspaper—that she'd really enjoyed. She realized that she wanted to be a writer, but she wasn't sure if this was a practical goal. She began talking with some of the people in her primary circle—most of them were lawyers or clients—and she received a good deal of positive reinforcement about her writing skills as well as sound advice. One piece of advice from a veteran networlder was that she needed to connect with people in the writing and journalism professions. Through referrals from people in her circle, Evelyn began interacting with an American Bar Association editor as well as a reporter for a local publication who had once interviewed her for a story about a case she was working on.

Both of these people soon became part of her networld, and they provided her with insights and ideas about how she might start a career in this new field. Through her exchanges with these people as well as a referral to someone else who had made an equally dramatic career change, Evelyn gained the confidence and contacts to make a move. Within six months, Evelyn found a job as a reporter for a newspaper in a suburb of Minneapolis. She was able to live in a small town where the cost of living was 30 percent lower than where she had been living. She had researched the school district and found the schools in the town to be exceptional, the community very involved and committed to keeping the town safe, and the people supportive of one another. She knew that the job on the paper was just a stepping-stone for her to grow a new career as a writer. For Evelyn, reassessing her goals was the best thing she could have done. Her evolving networld provided her with all the support (emotional, informational, knowledge, promotional, wisdom, and transformational opportunities) that she needed to make the transition into a new career.

Take the Test of Time

One of the simplest and easiest ways to evaluate your networld is by analyzing how you're spending your time when you're in it. For example, are you spending 80 percent of your Networlding time with four or five partners with whom you're continuously creating mutual opportunities? Or are you spending 80 percent of your time with one or two veterans in your primary circle but jointly creating very few opportunities with them? If the latter is true, you need to re-create your networld. This means taking any one of a number of actions: finding new people for your primary circle, moving people up from secondary and tertiary circles, attempting to target more influencers for your networld, and bridging divergent networlds. Temporarily, your time needs to be focused on re-creating rather than co-creating opportunities.

Your goal is to spend your Networlding time effectively (doing the right things) and efficiently (doing the right things right). In order to figure out where you are spending your time, once every six months take a moment to create a pie chart. Divide the pie into the people in your primary circle and assign a percentage of time you've spent with each over the past six-month period. Then write down what you've exchanged with each person: emotional support, information, and opportunities, such as referrals. Looking at this list, ask yourself the following questions:

- With whom am I spending the most time? And who is providing me with the most productive exchanges?
- Is someone in this circle providing the best exchanges in the least amount of time?
- Is someone providing the least rewarding exchanges in the most amount of time?
- Based on this six-month evaluation, am I spending my Networlding time in optimum ways to achieve my goals?

This evaluation will help you answer the critical question of whether you need to tinker with or re-create your primary circle (or whether it's fine as it is). It is helpful to do this evaluation at least twice a year to maintain the health of your circle. Many times, it will simply confirm what you intuitively know: it's time to make some changes.

Monitor and Maintain the Exchange Dynamic

Networlding relationships must constantly nurture exchanges. This isn't networking; you're not simply exchanging names randomly and intermittently. Just as you must continuously evaluate how your Networlding time is spent, you must do everything possible to maximize your exchanges. Seth Godin, author of the best-selling book *Permission Marketing* (1999), has emphasized strategies for staying in contact and adding value to relationships. He states that the only way for companies to secure trust and therefore loyalty among customers is through building mutually beneficial learning relationships over time. The same holds true for building strong Networlding relationships.

It takes commitment and creativity to build mutually productive exchanges, and this is a responsibility all Networlding partners must take seriously. To fulfill this responsibility, the first requirement is to keep in touch. Communicate with those in your primary circle at least once a month. Don't wait to be called. It won't happen at all or won't happen frequently enough for you to establish an ongoing exchange.

Second, design creative strategies to ensure that your exchanges continue to evolve. For example, create a time-sensitive agenda for your Networlding meetings that lists three or four questions or requests you have about opportunities you are currently exploring. Ask for similar questions or requests from your partner before going to the meeting. Having an agenda will ensure that you don't spend the meeting on one-sided exchanges. It will also help you maximize the time you spend together and focus on substantive issues rather than superficial ones. The following is a sample agenda.

Meeting time: 30 minutes.

Meeting: initiated by phone by Margaret.

Agenda:

11:00–11:05: Overview of current status of each partner.

11:05–11:15: Bill offers his current project interests: (1) looking for new employees for his growing department; (2) locating an organization that specializes in finance; (3) seeking alliance partners.

11:15–11:25: Margaret offers her current project interests: (1) investigating going for an MBA (looking for recommendations on schools); (2) seeking a mentor in another field: (3) looking for a new job at a company that might fund graduate school tuition.

11:25–11:30: Summarize and set time for next meeting.

During Bill and Margaret's discussion of their current project interests, each stimulates creative connections by asking questions such as these: Who would you connect with if you were looking [to change careers or find a good organization in my field or locate a mentor]? Do you know anyone who might be able to help me with [a given project or opportunity]? Who else in your circles might be good mentors? What would you suggest I do first?

Third, after you meet with your Networlding partner, evaluate what was exchanged. Were you satisfied with what you received? Was your partner happy with what you provided? Did either of you feel that the other fell short in a critical exchange area (that is, not enough good, solid information was exchanged)? What might you do to enhance the exchange next time you meet?

Sometimes it's possible that nothing you can do will enhance exchanges because of the changes that have been going on in both of your lives, and it may be a good idea to look to others as Networlding partners. In other instances, however, there may be a great deal to be gained by interacting with these people, and the key is to boost the quality and quantity of your exchanges.

Establish a Comfortable Work-Life Balance

One of the issues many established networlders have to deal with is too many opportunities. This may seem like a positive circumstance, but it can quickly become a negative one if your life is thrown out of balance. *Workaholism* is a danger, especially for people who have spent years trying to reach the point where opportunities exist for them. It's understandably difficult to turn down anything. Remember, however, that you won't maintain your networld just by grabbing opportunities. Part of the re-creating process is learning which opportunities to pursue and which to turn down.

Work-life balance means different things to different people at different stages of their careers. Liz Dolan was originally a vice president at Nike; she left the organization to develop a better work-life balance. Dolan St. Clair, the new organization she formed, is a marketing company that works with no more than three clients at a time. Liz is also involved in volunteer activities and a radio show with her four sisters. She created a more balanced work schedule after spending years at corporate jobs that required great amounts of time. She essentially turned down opportunities in an organization in favor of a different type of opportunity outside of one. She embodies the spirit of Networlding, which holds that the process isn't just for getting ahead but also for achieving fulfillment in all realms of one's life—work, family, and spiritual.

Evaluate each opportunity in terms of your goals and values. If one doesn't fit what you're hoping to achieve and what you believe, turn it down. Keep this saying in mind: "You can tell the sign of a successful person by the number of times he or she can say no." Say no to opportunities that don't fit into your scheduled time for your family or your personal life as well as ones that don't dovetail with your career goals. Networlders who say no to the many projects, jobs, and volunteer positions that are offered to them have more success in the meaningful areas of their lives; they give themselves the time to say yes to what they should say yes to.

When you are able to say no to the things that don't mesh with your strategic life goals, you will find yourself a much better evaluator of opportunities. You become more analytical and really stop and think before moving forward with a new project or taking a new job. Dan is a good example of someone who makes sure he only takes on opportunities that he can fully commit to because they are in alignment with his abilities, values, and vision. As the owner of a successful business, he regularly gets requests from his primary circle to pursue other opportunities involving new business start-ups. He's learned to say no to most of them, even though he's passed on some proposals that could have been extremely lucrative. Dan's Networlding rationale is that most of these other businesses not only involve areas he knows little about but also involve work he's not particularly interested in. His participation in these areas would take away time from his own business, which is both profitable and meaningful to him.

Saying no takes some practice. It's awkward at first to decline an opportunity, especially one presented to you by a valued Networlding partner. But you'll find that you can do so gracefully and honestly, and that others will respect you for your integrity and willingness to adhere to your principles.

Keep the Boundaries Fluid

When you begin Networlding, you will probably stick pretty close to home, linking up with people in your field or your friends and family. As much as you might want to broaden the scope of your primary circle, you may find it easier and more comfortable to focus on people who work at the same company as you or are in the same industry. But by the time you reach this step in the process, you should be ready to be more adventurous. By linking in ways that cross boundaries, you redefine your networld. Rather than a homogeneous entity, it becomes much more heterogeneous.

Kevin used to think that his networld should be self-contained and only involve those with whom he interacted daily. Yet like many accomplished networlders, Kevin became skilled at the process and decided to make connections across his particular boundary. Because he was a salesperson, his primary circle involved customers and other sales professionals. However, he wanted to consider career opportunities outside of his field, so he made an effort to connect with people outside of this narrow boundary. Through discussions with Doreen, a member of his primary circle, he hooked up with Larry, a top executive at another company. Larry and Kevin had a number of discussions about management positions in which a great deal of information and ideas were exchanged. Pretty soon, Larry was part of Kevin's primary circle and referred him to an executive at another company that had an opening for a young management trainee. Kevin was hired for the position and has moved up through management ranks. During this time, he re-created his networld to reflect his new career goals as well as his desire to lead a less hectic, more centered life.

To a certain extent, boundaries are natural. Everyone has areas of interest and goals that predispose them to find certain types of people for their networlds. At the same time, these boundaries can prove restrictive, especially after you've been Networlding for a while and are growing personally and professionally. At this point, you need to stop defining yourself and your connections by what you currently do and open up your networld to individuals who may be in completely different fields or leading very different lives from the one you're used to.

Continuously Extend the Connections

At this point in the process, you should not only think about your networld as an ever-changing, growing organism but also do everything possible to accelerate this growth. This means constantly looking for ways to extend your networld to new and diverse people in order to increase your primary circle's collective success. In other words, keep stretching your *horizon of observability*. Focus on each of your partner's distinct networks; they should be growing their groups just as you are growing yours. Each month, they will have developed a variety of new relationships with which you can connect. Ask questions like these: Who do you enjoy working with lately? Why? Both questions are useful. The first helps you identify particular individuals you could be introduced to and the second helps you match your interests, values, and goals with those that others might embrace.

For example, your primary circle partner says, "This month I was talking with a new colleague named Aaron. He is involved in a project to market a software product globally." You ask, "What organization does Aaron work for?" Your partner tells you, and it's a company you have been hoping to learn more about. As you inquire about Aaron's global software venture, you become increasingly intrigued. If your partner is sufficiently empathic, he'll realize you're interested in meeting Aaron. If he's not, you may have to ask directly if he'd mind setting up a meeting. When you meet Aaron, you realize that there's really no place for you in the project. But you and Aaron discover that you like and trust each other, that you have similar interests and ideas. Aaron mentions that Cynthia, a friend of his, is working on a similar project for another organization. You immediately express interest in talking to her. It may be that Cynthia will become a member of your networld or that Aaron will (or both of them will). It may be that Cynthia leads you to another person with whom you explore opportunities. As long as you keep extending your connections, you're bound to encounter people who will make good Networlding partners.

Be Open to New Types of Opportunities

It's easy to fall into an *opportunity rut*. In other words, you keep pursuing the same types of opportunities rather than exploring the variety to which you're introduced. Part of re-creating your networld
involves shifting your opportunities as your interests and goals shift.
Some people, however, cling to one particular opportunity type. For
instance, Jack was a young consumer electronics salesman, who as
his career progressed, became increasingly interested in the technical side of the business. In his spare time, he would experiment with
stereo components, attempting to rework them so they produced
better sound. His Networlding had helped him develop a strong
primary circle, and his career had benefited from the prospects he'd
been referred to by his circle partners. One of the people in his circle, Jim, recognized that Jack's interests were shifting and told him
about various programs that might help him develop skill in the
technical area; he even found out about a course at a local school
Jack could take to become a certified technician. But Jack constantly
turned down these and other opportunities that didn't relate to
sales. His position was that he didn't want to give up a career he'd
worked hard for and that provided him with an excellent salary.

Trade-offs are part of re-creating your networld. With every
opportunity you choose another will be tabled permanently or temporarily. This can involve difficult choices, especially if your career
or life is changing. It's difficult to give up money for more career satisfaction or the security of working with familiar people for the
insecurity of working with people you don't know well. Many times
the opportunity trade-offs involve short-term versus long-term
issues. Your boss is giving you an opportunity to do more traveling
and earn more money in the short term, but to achieve your long-
term goal you're considering your Networlding partner's sugges-
tion that you return to school and obtain an advanced degree.

To make the right trade-offs, you need to be clear about your
goals. As we emphasized earlier, you must reassess your objectives
regularly (at least once a year). Be intensely aware of what it is you
really want to achieve in your life. With that awareness, trade-offs
are easier to make (though they still may involve a difficult choice).

You also need to make time for new opportunities. If you try to
pursue all your existing projects, you won't have enough time or

energy to devote to new ones. In Networlding as in life, you can't have your cake and eat it too. Consciously decide what you're willing to give up so that you can focus on what's of utmost important in your work, career, and life.

Nancy followed this advice when she decided she would step away from a number of political obligations and instead focus on building a consulting business. For years, she had been heavily involved in local politics and that was her mission in life. But as she grew older, she became increasingly interested in business issues. Business consulting really turned her on, and she wanted to pursue opportunities to build her practice. At first, though, she resisted this impulse and the opportunities Networlding partners offered her. "I'm too old to change careers," she rationalized. "Politics was what I used to dream about doing, and it's hard to give it up." But political work was no longer her dream, and after a few discussions with one of her Networlding partners, Nancy mustered up the courage to take on a business consulting project. In doing so, she had to decline work on the election campaign of a state representative for whom she had worked many times in the past. It was difficult to say no to him and yes to the consulting work, but when she realized that consulting was what was most important to her at this stage in her life, she was able to choose.

Keep a Maintenance Checklist

Some networlders reach Step Seven and feel they can coast. They become confident in their ability to connect with others, find influencers, and exchange all types of support. In short, they believe great opportunities will continue to flow if they just maintain the status quo.

In fact, they have to maintain their networld's viability. They must inspect all the major components of their networld for wear and tear and replace what no longer works properly. We're not asking people to rebuild their networld from scratch continuously, but we are suggesting that they keep an eye out for problems. To that end, here is a maintenance checklist you'll find helpful:

1. Once a month, list your exchanges with your partners. Look at the Networlding support exchange model and determine if these exchanges continue to meet your goals.

2. Determine if your primary circle partners are also your friends. Unlike in networking, Networlding isn't all business. The trust and meaningful communication that are so essential to this process often results in friendship. If you find that you don't consider any of your Networlding partners your friends, this is a sign that something is wrong.

3. Every other month or so take time to think about those in your primary and secondary circles and ask yourself, "Should this person remain in that circle?" If your partners are not responding in satisfactory ways to your prearranged phone conferences or personal meetings, they are most likely not currently in a position to be good Networlding partners. Conversely, if you find you're having more meaningful exchanges with someone in your secondary circle than your primary one, move this person up.

4. Determine whether your Networlding partners are satisfied with the support and opportunities you're giving them. Networlding is not just about you. Even if you're satisfied, the process will be obstructed if your partners are not. Invariably, they will provide less and less support as their dissatisfaction increases. Therefore, talk to them about your Networlding partnership and encourage them to be honest about how they feel.

Position (or Reposition) Yourself as a Resource

Don't assume that everyone knows what you have to offer. People not only forget the variety of resources you offer them but sometimes are unaware when you develop a new area of experience and expertise. Therefore, make sure you keep those in your primary circle abreast of the projects you're working on and the new knowledge and skills you've developed. These can be significantly different a year or two into a relationship than they were when you first started Networlding.

Even if your skills and knowledge don't change significantly, you should use written, electronic, and verbal communication to remind people what you're involved in. We've found that the networlders who receive the most opportunities are those who are known as resource providers. They're the ones who everyone in the networld knows to call for specific types of assistance. In gratitude for this assistance and as part of the reciprocity that governs networld relationships, others respond with opportunities. Again, don't be shy about making your people connections, knowledge, and skills known to everyone in your networld. Don't brag about who or what you know, just communicate objectively what you've been doing and who you've been working with. People will immediately understand that you're broadcasting this knowledge to help them rather than just to help yourself.

Sometimes making networlders aware of your resources results in completely unexpected opportunities, as Carlotta discovered. She communicated her insurance industry expertise to others in her networld, and as a result was frequently asked for assistance on a wide variety of insurance-related projects. Sam worked for an organization that needed help writing business insurance proposals to large corporations, a particular strength of Carlotta's. When Sam called with this request, however, she was swamped, and furthermore, she didn't view his call as an opportunity she particularly wanted to pursue. But because he was in her primary circle, she was glad to share some ideas about how the proposals should be written. She was also honest about why she wasn't interested in taking on the project herself. She explained that she was spending whatever free time she had learning to play the guitar; her long-term goal was to write music and shift her career in that direction.

Sam surprised her by explaining that he had been playing the guitar for years and that if she would work with him on the project, he'd teach her how to play. Carlotta jumped at the chance. Since mastering the guitar, she has written a number of songs, one of which was recorded by a professional performer for an album.

Be Ambitious About Networlding

By this step in the process, you should have honed your abilities to the point that you can network with anyone. If you haven't included influencers in your circles by this point (and you should have at least some), then do so now. If you've been practicing the techniques suggested in this book, you are well-prepared to connect with the thought leaders and top performers in your field.

Create a list of the five industry influencers you would like to meet and communicate this list to everyone in your primary circle.

Although you may not be able to connect with all or most of them immediately, you certainly will be able to gain an introduction to one of them relatively soon.

Antoinette wanted to get in contact with a pioneering Chicago restaurateur, Rich Melman, on behalf of her parents, who owned a bakery. She was looking to help them grow their business by supplying Melman's Lettuce Entertain You restaurant chain with its bakery goods. One of the people in Antoinette's networld, Scott (he wasn't even in her secondary circle) thought of a friendship he had made with a marketing director at Michael Jordan's restaurant. Though Scott didn't have a connection that led directly to Melman, he was able to provide her (actually, her parents) with a referral that led to other prominent restaurant executives. If Antoinette and her parents continue this Networlding process, it will only be a matter of time before they will leverage their new connections and be introduced to Melman.

Know When a Relationship Should End

Networlders need to end relationships as well as start them. As your networld changes because of changes in your goals, you will have to communicate that a relationship is no longer viable. People we've worked with tell us that it's difficult to tell someone this without hurting their feelings and burning bridges. Determining when to move someone out of a primary circle can also be problematic.

There is no scientific formula that can guide your decision making in this regard. Still, here are the most common reasons for ending or changing Networlding relationships (that is, moving them to a secondary or tertiary circle):

- You or your partner (or both) shift your goals, and this shift makes it difficult if not impossible to create joint opportunities or refer relevant individuals to each other.
- Your partner's values change (or his true values emerge over time). You realize that you don't share the same ethics or that what's important in your universe is irrelevant to him. Many times, this shows up when you try to work on a project together and the way you work on it clashes (for example, he just wants to get it done, you want to get it done right).

- You realize there's a lack of reciprocity. Your partner is a taker and not a giver, and the lack of reciprocity triggers the relationship's end.

Monitor your own gut feelings about and behaviors toward other people in your networld. Are you not calling someone as much as you used to? Is that person not calling you? Do you find yourself hesitating to make a referral to this person or deciding not to refer people at all? Are you angry or frustrated when you try to create a joint opportunity?

Sometimes you just need to discuss these situations with a Networlding partner and clear the air. There may be a simple reason for what's been going on and you can resolve the issue quickly. In other instances, however, the change in your feelings and behaviors reflects a value or goal disconnect that means it's time for the relationship to change.

If this is the case, be honest and sensitive when you discuss your feelings. Don't accuse the other person of not holding up his or her end of things or of some other negative behavior. Perhaps in time this person will return to your primary circle because your interests and objectives will once again mesh. Therefore, be civil and complimentary. After all, at one point you felt there was a good match between you. Focus on the positives and thank the other person for his or her contributions. Although it's fine to address the reason for the rift, don't become embroiled in a pointless argument about who was responsible for the problems.

Also, be willing to reconnect at some point in the future. Yes, it may be awkward to do so but life has a funny way of both pulling relationships apart and putting them back together. We've known a number of Networlding partners who have ended relationships only to find a few years later that various events and circumstances made a reconnection feasible.

Make Lists and Check Them Twice

List making is an organizational and an opportunity tool. As we've already said, at this point in the process you're probably going to be meeting more people and encountering more opportunities than you know what to do with. For this reason, you should make lists that can help you keep these things straight.

One list should include all the potential projects, businesses, and so on that you might want to pursue. Write them all down and prioritize the list. What opportunity seems to match your values, mission, and goals best? What opportunity seems most ill-matched to your plans? You want to achieve top-of-mind awareness for your high-priority opportunities. In this way, you can constantly be on the lookout for people and projects that might move an opportunity toward fruition. With your list in mind and in hand, you'll remember to ask people you meet questions that are related to these opportunities.

Similarly, put together a list of people who are candidates for your primary circle. These may be people you've met once or twice or individuals you've heard about from others (or read about or heard speak). Creating this primary list will remind you to ask people in your networld about these individuals: Do they know them? What do they think of them? Can they refer you? It will also provide you with a reminder to contact these individuals and talk with them on the phone, send them e-mails, and arrange lunches and meetings.

As an experienced networlder, you need to intensify rather than step back from Networlding activities. With your experience, you should constantly work to strengthen your primary circle, and these lists are a simple way to help you do so.

Develop Networlding Savvy

When you're just starting out making connections and developing your circles, your objective is to learn the ropes and become comfortable with the process. But when you reach the point where you have a strong networld in place and you're re-creating elements of it, you need to be savvy about the subtleties and relationship-building techniques that help networlds roll along smoothly. As you shift from opportunity to opportunity and change Networlding partners, you need to make quick transitions to new people. This is going to be difficult if you haven't mastered the following techniques.

Provide Postreferral Feedback

How many times have you been given a lead or even a referral and not followed up on it? Make it a point to take leads and referrals seriously and to communicate results back to your networld partners. This is all about honoring others and communicating your understanding and appreciation of the effort it takes to make a referral or provide a lead. One executive director of a home health care agency says he remembers the few individuals who kept him informed through letters and phone calls of their success with the leads and the referrals he provided. In fact, he chose one of the young men who was especially good at staying connected over the years to become the head of operations when his chief operating officer left. Acknowledging other people's gifts to us is part of an ongoing exchange. It increases the odds that your networld partners will continue to provide you leads and referrals, because you obviously appreciated the ones they provided in the past.

Control Your Impulse to Push a Relationship

Networlders aren't pushy, though they certainly are proactive and assertive. This may seem to be a fine line, but it's an important distinction. It's not pushy to ask a primary circle partner for a lead or referral; it is pushy to ask over and over again. As you're re-creating your networld, you're going to be interacting with people with whom you don't have a track record. If you're overly pushy, they may believe they've made a mistake and drop out of your circle. Learn to read your partners quickly and take a cue from their body language as well as their verbal responses. If you ask them what happened to that business idea they mentioned the last time and you see them stiffen, it's a good idea to back off. Be diplomatic in your approach. Rather than push him toward it, ask leading questions that allow your partner to pull you toward an issue. For instance, if you're eager to attend a conference as a guest of your partner, ask, "Have you made plans yet to attend the conference? It sounds like there are going to be a number of terrific speakers." Don't say, "I'd really like to go with you to the conference," unless you're reasonably sure this will be fine with your partner.

Develop the Skill and Reputation for Keeping Confidences

When Anthony shared his confidential information with Norma and no one else, he did so because Norma had a reputation for keeping confidences. She was well known in her office and among her primary circle as someone who could be trusted to be discreet. As a result, Norma was more tuned in to what was going on in her networld than anyone else. If you can develop a similar reputation, you'll find that you become a magnet not only for information but for other people. Everyone has a secret, and everyone has a need to tell this secret to someone they trust. As you reconstruct your networld, information will be your best building material. As someone with a reputation for keeping confidences and possessing a great deal of inside knowledge, you'll find it that much easier to form new Networlding relationships. Re-creating your networld won't be a formidable task because people gravitate toward you.

Develop Networlding Maturity

Being savvy means staying attuned to the nuances of the Networlding process. However, being mature requires you to be reflective, strategic, and wise. As you become skilled at this process and re-create your networld in more ambitious ways, you'll need to develop a level of maturity appropriate to the objectives you're trying to achieve. You can no longer charge headlong after each opportunity that comes your way, for example. It may be fine to do so when you're just starting out, but now you need to be more analytical and assess your opportunities carefully. At this stage, you may need to invest more time, money, and other resources in an opportunity, and you don't want to do so without some careful consideration. Here are the elements of what we define as maturity:

Learn Not to Do Everything Yourself

The trick here is using Networlding as a form of delegation. As you build stronger and better networlds, the demands on your time will increase. You're going to have to prioritize what you can and should do versus what you can't and shouldn't do. We've found that mature networlders exchange low-priority tasks with people in their secondary and tertiary circles in return for advice, referrals, and the chance to participate in opportunities. This is a fair exchange because you're gaining valuable time to concentrate on the most important opportunities and you're giving someone else (usually a younger person with less experience) a chance to learn and grow.

Slow Down to Speed Up

This bit of advice may seem contradictory. But in fact, as you restructure your connections and pursue new goals, you must take a breath and reflect before moving forward. By choosing your opportunities more carefully and slowly, you increase the odds that they're the right ones for you. Though it may take you a bit longer to move forward, once you make your decision you'll reach your destination faster (because you made the right choice). You may be a hare when you start Networlding, but you should shift to tortoise mode later on.

Work to Strengthen Relationships Even During a Breakdown

A few paragraphs back we talked about the need to know when to end relationships. At the same time, mature networlders don't end relationships prematurely. We've found that as people re-create their networlds, the process makes waves. As you shift your gaze to new goals and look for new ways to pursue fresh opportunities, you will see more of some primary circle partners and less of others. This may cause a certain amount of animosity, and if you value a relationship and still see it as crucial in your re-created networld, you need to use rifts as leverage to strengthen these relationships. Arrange a meeting with the partners who are upset, and talk about the issues. Be honest. Describe your new goals, what you're trying to achieve, and most important, why you believe it will be mutually beneficial to maintain the relationship.

When relationships break down, one strategy for repair is to go back to the time the relationship started and review what brought you together. This advice comes from Jackie Sloane, president of Sloane Communications in Chicago a successful marketing consultant and coach. When one of her clients missed five appointments in a row, she stopped all her work with that company and said, "I really enjoy working with you. Your company is great. You wanted me to help you distinguish the company in the marketplace and there have been some breakdowns lately. What I know from experience is that it is very difficult to do my job or provide value to you if there is no trust, if there is no flow of communication. That's what was so great about our relationship from the very beginning." Through a heart-to-heart, truth-telling talk, Jackie initiated a repair of a relationship that would otherwise have ended badly.

Re-create Your Networld with High-Potential Relationships

As you grow as a networlder, you need to aim higher in your relationships with your primary circle partners. Ask them, "What is the highest potential we both can reach?" When you encourage your partners to visualize where the relationship can grow you drive the energy of your relationship. One networlder named Sandra shared this idea with a primary partner named Gavin. Gavin was very interested in writing a book. He had held his position as a director of knowledge management for his Fortune 500 organization for the past three years and had refined a process that was very successful. Sandra, an external consultant and author of business books, had strengths that were complementary to Gavin's knowledge-management expertise. During one Networlding session the two explored the highest potential of their relationship and came to realize that they could create a book together. This collaborative effort was beyond Gavin's experience and seemed like a pipe dream at first. But Sandra saw the possibilities and worked to help Gavin see them. Both of them were redefining their goals and re-creating their networlds, and the book would help them both achieve their new goals. As a result of their discussion, they began working on a book on the growing business of knowledge management.

In sum, as you re-create your networld and interact with old and new partners, don't settle for "ordinary" relationships. Push the relationship potential to its limit. If your values are in synch and your goals and missions match up, you can set your sights high without fear. When you do, you will evolve to a more universal view of yourself, your networld, and your opportunities.

CHAPTER TEN

Thriving in the Networlding Universe

To succeed in our new connected economy, you must think and act in a new way. As the preceding chapters have made clear, Networlding requires a different approach to establishing and leveraging relationships in order to attain transformational opportunities. It's not only how you act toward people but also how you think about your relationships. If you're able to think and act like a networlder—connecting intentionally; being aware of your values, mission, and goals; identifying influencers; and so on—you can create amazing joint opportunities with others. These opportunities are wide-ranging, helping you achieve goals ranging from a career shift to growth in an organization to entrepreneurial success.

However, Networlding is more than this. As you embark on a Networlding path and see how connected you really are to an incredibly diverse group of people and opportunities, you'll realize that it is more than just a way of achieving career success. You'll come to understand that Networlding is a way of life.

Your old perspectives and beliefs will change as you adapt to the realities of a connected economy. Biases and boundaries that previously guided your thinking will disappear. As you begin exchanging resources and collaborating on opportunities, you'll discover that you are evolving. You'll become a member of the Networlding universe, able to form relationships and achieve goals with astonishing ease and speed. At a certain point, you won't have to think about Networlding. It will become a reflex, a natural way of relating to the connected world around you.

Being a Member of the Universe

Lois Weisberg, the seventy-four-year-old commissioner of cultural affairs for the city of Chicago, seems to be attuned to the connectedness of this universe. She has developed the Networlding reflex.

Lois is the kind of person who knows everyone. In and of itself, this doesn't make her a Networlding expert, though. What elevates her to that level is what she does with her connections. She exchanges information, ideas, emotional support, and wisdom with a wide circle of people, a circle she seems to re-create continuously. To her, there are no people boundaries; she is willing to start a conversation and make a connection in all sorts of environments to create new opportunities. According to a wonderful story in *The New Yorker,* Lois was driving down the street one day when she saw city workers about to cart away a beautiful sculpture from a public park. At that moment, she noticed a young woman, with a bundled-up baby in her arms, protesting their action. Lois, who had just started the Friends of the Parks organization, immediately got out of her car and began questioning the woman, who explained how much she liked the sculpture. A relationship blossomed, and the woman soon became the president of Friends of the Park and served in this capacity for the next ten years.

Gallery 37 is another Lois Weisberg project that demanded bringing diverse groups of people together. The program provides everything from a downtown gallery to various forms of support for lower-income and middle-class kids who are interested in art. Lois brought together federal bureaucrats, city agencies, real estate people, artists, and the schools to create Gallery 37. It has been so successful at fostering interest in the arts among public school children that it has been copied in cities throughout the world.

To create opportunities with others, Lois doesn't use power or position. Instead, she relies on her mastery of the connections that already exist. She just sees them and facilitates them better than anyone else. This is the powerful process of Networlding.

Redefining Boundaries and Risks

Lois is obviously the exception to the rule. Most of us possess certain beliefs concerning our separateness from others based on several factors, including race, organization, affiliations, country of residence, and so on. We have comfortable notions about boundaries that define the arena in which we are willing to develop meaningful relationships and new opportunities. Under this scenario, we carefully select and build our networld to achieve our immediate intent or short-term goal. This approach, however, produces an exclusive rather than inclusive circle, and it limits our Networlding capacity.

Boundaries are contrary to the organic nature of organizations and governments in the twenty-first century. John Henry Clippenger in *The Biology of Business* hypothesizes that our connected economy is a world in which we organize and act like living systems. Ideas move organically from individual to individual, expanding and reorganizing in ever-growing circles and producing unexpected results at an exponential rate. Thus, a connected entity—which most closely resembles the structure of living organisms—becomes the preferred organizational model for our governments, businesses, and communities. Those people and nations that emulate the new biological order for globally advancing knowledge, technology, economies, and themselves will thrive.

Networlding too is an organic system that leverages our new connectedness to help us achieve our goals. It is not an end in itself, however, but rather a vehicle to take us to our destination: the Networlding universe. This is a place where large-scale opportunities are at our fingertips. When we reach this place in our minds, we take off all the artificial limitations on what we can achieve for ourselves and for others.

In one sense, removing boundaries is risky. It's uncomfortable at first to interact with people in different fields or of different nationalities. It's awkward to work with someone who has radically different ideas and perspectives than we do. The risk is that we're subjecting our own beliefs to scrutiny. When we work with new and different people, they will challenge us directly by confronting us or indirectly by putting forward their ideas. We risk having to change our minds and admit that we may not have been right or are no longer right.

But this risk is nothing compared with the risk of continuing to operate within our narrow boundaries. In a Networlding universe, we take a great risk when we limit our ideas and opportunities. As the world changes—as our goals and opportunities change—we're stuck with contacts that are virtually useless. We haven't broadened our connections to the point where we can move our careers or businesses in any direction we choose. Thus, as people evolve toward a Networlding universe, they begin to redefine their concept of risk.

Moving Toward a Universal Focus

As we have stated repeatedly, although networlders aren't selfless they do move beyond the selfishness that often characterizes networking. The universal focus of this process allows people to expand beyond personal intent to more universal themes of responsibility for one another. Even the more skeptical among us admit that we are evolving in this direction. In *The Dilbert Future,* satirical humorist Scott Adams concedes that despite the occasional idiot whose intentions may tend to "screw up" our new environment in which thoughts and intent determine our experiences, the current evolutionary state is "the beginning of something better." This "something better" is a world in which we will be able to define reality in a more direct way than we ever imagined possible.

Although this may seem like a utopian concept to some, experienced networlders realize that it is actually an emerging reality. They've seen how their interconnected relationships have enabled them to expand their mission and goals to include socially important concerns; how their values have changed to be other-directed rather than just inner-directed. To paraphrase Ralph Waldo Emerson, we move toward our dreams with the grace of a higher order of being. Similarly, we move beyond simple Networlding into the sphere of the Networlding universe.

Let's describe what this universe holds for you. Imagine meeting a friend for coffee and sharing with her your latest passion. You're upset about the closing of the neighborhood youth center, and you're determined to do something about it. The guy at the next table overhears your conversation. He tells you that his sister, a community organizer who lives in a city two thousand miles away, successfully fought city hall when a similar situation occurred there. You exchange information, and he tells you that he too is upset about what's happening and would be glad to work with you in any way possible to keep the center open. He's a lawyer, and he says he'll provide legal support for your efforts and that his sister will probably be glad to lend her assistance too. Seemingly in a few minutes your networld has expanded into a multidimensional alliance of creative collaboration. You have access to ideas and resources on a large scale. Together you develop a plan that saves the center. The experience is energizing and meaningful. You discover you have a talent for organizing and planning this type of effort. Just as important, you find it is far more rewarding than your regular job. With the help of your new Networlding partners, you begin to chart a course toward a new career.

We don't mean to say that all networlders must become community activists, missionaries, or social workers. What we mean is that in a Networlding universe, you may make the transition to a new career or a meaningful work experience just as in this anecdote—merely by talking about a cherished idea in a restaurant. Such connections often happen instantly and incredibly.

But you have to be prepared for this universe. If not, you'll distrust the person who overhears your conversation and not take what he says seriously. Then nothing will happen. The sooner you begin preparing, the sooner you can take advantage of all the hidden interconnectedness in your world. The Networlding universe is not a vision of the distant future but what's emerging right now.

The universe has a spiritual side, one that many networlders remark upon. When you internalize the principles of Networlding, you become open to new people in new ways. Rather than closing yourself off to someone because of what he does or only connecting with him on one level, you're able to achieve a much deeper connection. It may be with someone in Sudan. It may be with the CEO of one of the world's largest companies or a pioneering labor leader. It may be with someone fifty years older than you are. And it may reach the point that you understand the other person's concerns, complementary strengths, values, and mission in life. Knowing each other on all these levels, you work together with tremendous speed and efficiency.

Your ultimate intent in this universe centers on what the Dalai Lama, the exiled spiritual leader of the Tibetan people, refers to as *the universal goals*. These universal goals are happiness or contentment, appeasement of suffering, and meaningful relationships.

Because these basic goals are present in all of us, everyone you meet offers the possibility of a valuable exchange and the creation of a new opportunity.

We'd like to give you a sense of the Networlding universe by describing some networlders who have taken relationships, exchanges, and opportunities to an extremely high level. We want to give you a sense of the potential in each of these three categories, beginning with relationships.

Seeking Relationships That Transcend Boundaries

Transcending the limitations that prevent most relationships from reaching their potential is the ideal goal of a Networlding universe. To approach this ideal, you need to transform your thinking. Unconsciously or consciously, most of us "rule out" people from participating in our networlds. They're too young or too old, too influential or not influential enough; they practice the wrong politics; they are from a different culture; they're employed by a competitor. The list goes on and on.

The formal Networlding process presented in these pages will help you transform your thinking. It makes you conscious of ruling people out because of petty distinctions (and helps you recognize that you should only rule people out for meaningful reasons, like a clash in values). The process helps you become intentional. As many networlders tell us, after practicing these techniques over a period of time, they internalize the process and it becomes second nature.

This universal ideal mandates incredibly diverse relationships, and Roberta is someone who embodies this ideal. Using her Networlding approach, she's achieved professional fulfillment and personal happiness. Roberta's passion was sewing lace. A few years ago she searched the Internet for the best sources of material. In doing so, she contacted many suppliers and other lace enthusiasts from all over the world. When an Internet correspondent had a question about the appropriate use and handling of a particular lace, Roberta would always find the answer. Sometimes the communication was difficult, because those Roberta interacted with spoke different languages and used lace in different ways. But because of her patience with others, Roberta exchanged information and support that enabled her to develop strong relationships. She didn't reject people because they didn't know much about lace or because they were from another country. She treated young, beginning lace enthusiasts with the same respect and support as she did veteran suppliers. Roberta's communication, openness, knowledge, and initiative helped her to create a joint opportunity with the others.

This universal lace circle decided to create an electronic newsletter to exchange information and new ideas. Roberta's generosity was further rewarded by many invitations to visit her new international friends, and a request by a magazine editor to write a regular column.

Roberta is emblematic of the new networld universe in more ways than one. She has not only been able to transcend the boundaries that hold others back in their relationships but also made excellent use of the Internet as a Networlding tool. With her networld universe perspective alone, Roberta could never have achieved the same results the old-fashioned way. Like any good networlder, she used the full power of the support exchange model, including exchanging basic information support and emotional support that eventually led to opportunities. What distinguishes Roberta is that she had an almost innate ability to transcend boundaries in her relationships. As a result, she quickly developed an amazingly divergent networld.

Seeking a Higher Level of Exchange

The Networlding universe goes far beyond traditional information sharing and knowledge transfers. It entails giving and receiving wisdom. Rooted in experience and shaped by expertise and feelings, wisdom is a tremendously valuable gift. In some ways, it's more valuable than any opportunity, referral, or lead. Wisdom can help you understand how and what opportunities to pursue; it can provide insight about how to reach key influencers; it can put your life in perspective and spur the reflection necessary to reprioritize your activities. In short, wisdom cuts to the heart of the matter and helps you see personal and professional issues more clearly.

Lisa and Victor are Networlding partners, and both are entrepreneurs. Lisa has a gardening catalogue business and Victor owns a restaurant. For a number of years, Victor's restaurant did very well, but in the last year business began to fall off because of increased competition in the area. He tried a number of approaches to revive it—hiring a new chef, increasing his advertising, and so on—but nothing worked. When Lisa and Victor first talked about the problem, Lisa offered terrific information, such as articles about restaurant marketing as well as a referral to a consultant who had helped her a few years back. Victor read the information and talked to the consultant but none of it seemed to have much of an impact. Lisa and Victor continued to meet regularly, and Lisa dedicated herself to providing Victor with something useful to help him deal with these critical issues. She and Victor had developed a friendship as well as a Networlding partnership, and so she thought long and hard about the options available to him.

One night after her children had gone to bed and she was reading, an idea came to Lisa. Victor needed to expand his business. It was exactly what Lisa had done when her gardening catalogue's profits had nosedived a few years back. She'd realized that she was losing customers to bigger catalogues with more diverse offerings. Thus, she diversified, using her own networld to find new sources and increase the range of gardening tools, seeds, and services she offered. Lisa knew that there was a small store adjacent to Victor's restaurant that was unoccupied: What if he opened a takeout business in that space? He could use her pots to package the food, keeping it warm and making it easy to reheat. She immediately called Victor and shared her idea. He loved it, and in turn he suggested that he include a coupon in each pot for a free plant from Lisa's store. Six months later, Victor had a thriving takeout business and Lisa had a whole new group of customers.

Lisa and Victor exchanged wisdom with each other. Lisa had given Victor an insight about his business that had emotional, knowledge, and informational components. This was a revelation for Victor, and it literally changed the way he thought about his business and Lisa's.

Creating Exponential Opportunities

Perhaps the most amazing experience of the Networlding universe is creating exponential opportunities. These are opportunities that start in one place and expand outward in different directions.

Because of the interconnectedness of the world and your ability to tap into these connections, you and your partners turn a one-dimensional opportunity into a multidimensional opportunity. This doesn't just mean taking a small business and turning it into a big one. Exponential opportunities can take many forms, as Edward discovered.

A successful businessman and entrepreneur, Edward wanted to launch a school that would enhance inner-city students' academic performance using innovative teaching and computer communication technology. He had a strong vision, but he lacked teaching credentials and possessed only limited financial resources. Although Edward was reluctant to ask for help, he realized that to make this school a reality he would have to step outside his comfort zone and approach a broad array of people. Edward put his Networlding skills to work.

He began by identifying individuals who shared the desire to help create an exciting new school concept—people in his primary, secondary, and tertiary circles as well as "outsiders" he'd heard of or read about. He needed to exchange his dreams and hard work with those who could provide the expertise and support he required for the school. He began expanding his network to include academicians, community leaders and organizations, business representatives, and local government officials. Edward formed a powerful coalition that resulted in Smart School Charter Middle School, a public school of three hundred students that is operated by a private organization in Florida.

But the opportunities for Edward extended far beyond his charter school. As his relationships broadened and he began exchanging the wisdom he had gained in this area, related opportunities opened up. All sorts of exciting projects came Edward's way that allowed him to fulfill his mission of becoming an advocate for educating inner-city kids.

Monitoring Your Ability to Networld at the Highest Level

Realistically, it's probably unfair to expect anyone to networld at full potential all the time. Yet it is something everyone can strive for, and in a Networlding universe it is a goal that all of us should attempt to attain. Even if we fall short, we should be aware of what's possible. The following questions are designed to foster this awareness about your relationships, exchanges, and opportunities:

- Is your networld diverse in terms of age, race, religion, occupation, expertise, and experience?
- Are you able to overcome ingrained prejudices or predispositions to make your networld all-inclusive?
- Do the people in your primary circle resemble you (in age, profession, nationality, and so on) or are they more diverse?
- As you re-create your networld, do you add people who are different from or the same as those who were in it before?
- Do you believe you frequently exchange wisdom with people in your primary circle or does the exchange usually revolve around a different type of support?
- Are you likely to offer wisdom to your partners but they don't reciprocate (or vice versa)?
- Do you feel your wisdom is limited by your experience or by your reluctance to offer wisdom to your partner (because your partner might feel you're speaking out of turn or being pretentious)?
- Have you talked with your partner about the need to exchange wisdom and agreed that doing so would increase the value of your exchanges?
- When you create joint opportunities with others, do they lead somewhere (or remain focused on the initial opportunity)?
- Do you feel you're open to opportunity possibilities, that you're willing to follow opportunities wherever they lead?
- Do you define opportunities narrowly (short-term, profit-focused, industry-based) or narrowly and broadly (long-term, socially responsible, cross-industry)?

Hold your Networlding actions up to the light of these questions. The more you do, the better your Networlding will be.

Shaping Your Connected Future

As you enter the Networlding universe armed with the skills of this powerful process, the real question is this: What are you going to do with it? Are you just going to focus on the opportunities in front of you? Or are you going to rally your network to achieve more meaningful goals?

It's not that your career or work goals are unimportant; they're obviously crucial and should be part of your Networlding strategy. Networlders, however, learn to think in bigger, broader terms. They realize that they are responsible not only for what they can achieve but for what their partners' can accomplish; they understand that their entire network and all the connected networlds can be harnessed to shape some larger aspect of our world.

In *The Long Boom*, leading futurists Peter Schwartz, Peter Leyden, and Joel Hyatt characterize our transition to the twenty-first century as a full shift into a high-speed, innovative economy in which business approaches and capital markets structures are transformed (1999). The result is a dynamic global economy where geographic, political, and economic boundaries are blurred in the pursuit of ever-expanding technical and scientific advances. The authors believe that these advances facilitate or require connected relationships and new opportunities for people in every region of the world.

If they are right, then you and your network are in an enviable position in the opportunistic climate of the long boom economy. You have the Networlding ability to capture significant opportunities. But do you capture the opportunities and benefits for your network alone? Or do you have a higher level of responsibility? If you choose to look holistically at our new connected economy, the answer is undeniably that you have a higher level of responsibility.

This has certainly proven true in our experiences. As we researched and interviewed networlders, we saw that many of them had taken this process and expanded it beyond their "closed" group. They had applied the process for socially significant purposes, from cleaning up the environment to improving the educational system to feeding the hungry. They capitalized on their connectedness for society at large.

In our own work, we've attempted to use Networlding in socially responsible ways. Collaborating with the Focused Web Group (www.focusedweb.com), we developed the Networlding Web site (www.networlding.com) and invited socially responsible businesses to list their information. We knew that this would facilitate creative collaborations between organizations and individuals, spawning many innovative opportunities. It is our vision that a portion of all revenues generated from this Web site will be used to support the creation of opportunities for nonprofit, community-based networlds.

In this way, we intend to realize higher-level benefits. As you'll learn, the real payoff for working and living in the Networlding universe goes far beyond the many opportunities you create with others. The process gives you the chance to be successful and the chance to help others become successful. You can and should define "others" broadly; they can include people in your primary, secondary, and tertiary circles as well as all types of people in the world around you. When you interact with people as a true networlder, you not only reap professional rewards but also understand that you've made the world a better place both for people you know and for people in need.

Glossary: Networld Speak

Networld Speak is a lexicon that offers both new terms we created and preexisting terms for better communicating in our new connected society. Most of these terms, but not all, have been used in the book. Enjoy using them in your conversations and explore new ones yourself that make sense. Feel free to e-mail us at *melissa@ networlding.com* with new terms you create.

Bridger: An individual who is particularly adept at developing connections between two people who have just met. For example, a bridger will introduce Person A to Person B, sharing to both their common interests.

Co-create: The art and practice of two networlders developing opportunities that are mutually beneficial. For example, two networlders who develop a joint opportunity such as starting a company or developing a strategic alliance.

Community: People opting to be part of a relationship to a common whole. In on-line environments community is one of the key elements in achieving successful corporate knowledge sharing and e-businesses.

Conscious conversations: Thinking, focusing, and directing conversation around adding value and connection. Questions such as "How can I support this person?" and "What conversation can we engage in that will hold mutual benefit?" become part of our regular exchanges with others.

Covisioning: The process of blending one's own vision with someone else's to create new, unique opportunities.

Dialogue: A session that combines sharing all elements of the Networlding support exchange model. Dialogue implies more than a simple back-and-forthness of messages in interaction; it points to a particular process and quality of communication in which the participants "meet," which allows for changing and being changed.

Drift: The natural decline of an untended network. Networks require constant attention and connection or members drift to other relationships.

Exchange: A reciprocal giving and receiving of ideas, information, and support between individuals in the course of conversations between networlders.

Horizon of observability: The foreseeable number of people connected to those whom we meet. For example, you meet someone named Joe and Joe mentions his friend Anne. We usually have difficulty thinking about the people Anne knows, and so on. In reality, however, most of us have hundreds of relationships, and those people have hundreds, and so on. In other words, although we can't see them, we are connected to millions through our relationships with even just a few people.

Hot link: The support given by a member of a networld circle to another promoting that person's credibility. For example, John calls Julie on behalf of George, who Julie has not met yet, but John thinks she should meet him and develop strong network ties.

Human capital: The aggregation of top networlders within your primary, secondary, and tertiary circles.

Influencer: A person who has the ability to impact others.

Intellectual capital: The product of a networld that shares knowledge.

Knowledge: Information that is put to use. It contains the addition of experience in its context.

Leverage: The process of identifying and sustaining a focus on implementing pivotal strategies that accelerate the attainment of a desired outcome. Leveraging catalyzing relationships and opportunities that already exist to realize results yields better and faster outcomes.

Links: The distinguishing feature of the new network society. They represent the relationships one networlder has with another.

Maestro: An individual who creates a veritable orchestration of opportunities through linking people from divergent backgrounds and circles. The core person of a very active network creating a "hub" of activity.

Mapping: The process of assessing a person's talents, interests, and availability to participate in a Networlding opportunity.

Network: A system or process that involves a number of persons, groups, or organizations. Every network looks different.

The networked world: The new society that offers the ability to get information any time, any place—to buy things, receive medical care, use government services, bank on-line, and so on. The freedom to do everything that once required multiple steps, in fewer steps.

Networld: A combination of a primary, a secondary, and a tertiary circle or network. Networlders have one primary circle with no more than ten participants at any one time.

Networlder: A person who orchestrates people's talents, interests, and values to leverage the power of our networked world. A networlder is wonderful at matching people from divergent networks and connecting them to powerful, mutually beneficial opportunities.

Networlding: The process of developing long-term, mutually beneficial relationships and opportunities through a powerful support exchange model to achieve personal and professional lifelong fulfillment.

Networlding support exchange model: A hierarchy of support we can offer to those with whom we wish to build relationships that lead to fulfillment and opportunities. The model shows how we move from an initial level of exchanging emotional support to informational support, then to knowledge (where we also share personal experiences), to promotional support, and to wisdom to achieve transformational opportunities and fulfillment—the result of a growing relationship.

On-line community networks: Networks resulting in the creation of some kind of "on-line presence" that is a reflection of their particular community. Ultimately, though, the most exciting aspect of community networking is not really the systems themselves, but the *people* who are brought together and the *synergies* that happen around their projects. A group of people sharing common interests, ideas, and feelings over the Internet.

Pareto Principle: Named after Vilfredo Pareto, a nineteenth-century economist and sociologist, the Pareto Principle states that a small number of causes are responsible for a large percentage of the effect—usually a 20 percent to 80 percent ratio.

Participation: Networlds are webs of participation. At the heart of a successful networld are its members.

Path of greatest opportunity: The best possible connection of people and opportunities for Networlding. The focus is on what can be.

Peripheral talk: Conversation that is not directly focused on the topic at hand, yet is marginally connected and introduced to develop unique and creative connections.

Points of commonality: Comments in a conversation regarding the interests one networlder shares with another.

Points of credibility: Comments in a conversation that modestly and honestly communicate your accomplishments.

Primary circle: Ten people who are influencers with whom you have an ongoing exchange from the Networlding support exchange model. The ten in your primary circle should yield one hundred connections with other influencers from those in your primary circle's circle.

Relationship momentum: Networlds create more and better relationships as networlders connect from one powerful relationship to the next.

Salons: Homey places of connection centered around good conversation that herald back to the 1920s, when some very effective networking was done in the arts community. Today salons are back and growing in interest among people of all ages who enjoy conversation as one of life's greatest treasures. In a salon, a host is present to help connect people and facilitate conversation and knowledge sharing— a new twist on those who wish to leverage the Information Age.

Secondary circle: This network comprises those people who are always positioned to move into your primary network. Depending on the number of opportunities you are currently exploring or working on, the number of people in this network can become rather large—somewhere in the hundreds. Of course this also depends on how well you can maintain connection with these people. The Internet has made this much more possible.

Tertiary circle: The most distant of networks with people whom you communicate with very sporadically, for example, those to whom you only send holiday cards or connect with when you are in need of introductions, as is the case when job hunting.

Unifying purpose: This is the glue and the driver for the networld. Common views, values, and goals hold a networld together, while a shared focus on desired results keeps a network in synch and on track.

References

Adams, S. *The Dilbert Future: Thriving on Business Stupidity in the 21st Century.* New York: HarperBusiness, 1998.

Andreeva, N. "Do the Math—It Is a Small World: A Formula That Can Make Complex Organizations Simpler and More Efficient Grabs Attention." *Business Week,* Aug. 17, 1998, 54–55.

Clippenger, J. H. III. *The Biology of Business: Decoding the Natural Laws of Enterprise.* San Francisco: Jossey-Bass, 1999.

Conlon, J. K., and Giovagnoli, M. *The Power of Two: How Companies of All Sizes Can Build Alliance Networks That Generate Business Opportunities.* San Francisco: Jossey-Bass, 1998.

De Bono, E. *Serious Creativity: Using the Power of Lateral Thinking to Create New Ideas.* Des Moines, Iowa: Advanced Practical Thinking, 1993.

Freeman, L. "The Impact of Computer Based Communication on the Social Structure of an Emerging Scientific Specialty." *Social Forces,* June 1984.

Giovagnoli, M. *Angels in the Workplace: Stories and Inspirations for Creating a New World of Work.* San Francisco: Jossey-Bass, 1999.

Gladwell, M. "Six Degrees of Lois Weisberg." *The New Yorker,* Jan. 11, 1999, 52–63.

Godin, S. *Permission Marketing: Turning Strangers into Friends and Friends into Customers.* New York: Simon & Schuster, 1999.

Goleman, D. *Working with Emotional Intelligence.* New York: Bantam Books, 1998.

Guare, J. *Six Degrees of Separation.* New York: Vintage, 1990.

Krebs, V. "Visualizing Human Networks." *Ester Dyson's Monthly Report,* Feb. 12, 1996, 1–3.

Schwartz, P., Leyden, P., and Hyatt, J. *The Long Boom: A Vision for the Coming Age of Prosperity.* Reading, Mass.: Perseus, 1999.

Turner, C., and Webber, A. *All Hat and No Cattle: Tales of a Corporate Outlaw: Shaking up the System and Making a Difference at Work.* Reading, Mass.: Perseus, 1999.

Whitney, D., and Giovagnoli, M. *75 Cage-Rattling Questions to Change the Way You Work: Shake-Em-Up Questions to Open Meetings, Ignite Discussion, and Spark Creativity.* New York: McGraw-Hill, 1997.

Walker, C. "Word of Mouth", *American Demographics,* July 1995.

Index

Join networlding.com!

We invite you to subscribe to our free newsletter on Networlding. Signing up for it at our Web site: www.networlding.com. If you are committed to being socially responsible—in other words, to being a networlder—we also offer you a free directory listing so that you can networld with other networlders.